THE LIFE OF JESUS CHRIST

IN THE JAMES STALKER TRILOGY

THE LIFE OF JESUS CHRIST

James Stalker

ZondervanPublishingHouse
Grand Rapids, Michigan

A Division of HarperCollinsPublishers

THE LIFE OF JESUS CHRIST
Copyright © 1983 by The Zondervan Corporation
Grand Rapids, Michigan

Requests for information should be addressed to:
Zondervan Publishing House
Academic and Professional Books
Grand Rapids, Michigan 49530

Library of Congress Cataloging in Publication Data

Stalker, James, 1848–1927
    The life of Jesus Christ.

    1. Jesus Christ—Biography—Study. I. Title.
BT307.S76   1983   232.9'01   83-19794
ISBN 0-310-44191-9

Printed in the United States of America

94   95   96 / EP / 13   12   11   10

CONTENTS

1

THE BIRTH, INFANCY, AND YOUTH OF JESUS

1. THE NATIVITY

1. Augustus was sitting on the throne of the Roman empire, and the touch of his finger could set the machinery of government in motion over almost all the civilized world. He was proud of his power and wealth, and it was one of his favorite occupations to compile a register of the populations and revenues of his vast dominions. So he issued an edict, as the Evangelist Luke says, "that all the world should be taxed," or, to express accurately what the words probably mean, that a census, to serve as a basis for future taxation, should be taken of all his subjects. One of the countries affected by this decree was Palestine, whose king, Herod the Great, was a vassal of Augustus. It set the whole land in motion; for, in accordance with ancient

7

Jewish custom, the census was taken, not in the places where the inhabitants were at the time residing, but in the places to which they belonged as members of the original twelve tribes.

2. Among those whom the edict of Augustus drove from a distance to the highways was a humble pair in the Galilean village of Nazareth—Joseph, the carpenter of the village, and Mary, his espoused wife. They had to travel nearly a hundred miles in order to be inscribed in the proper register; for, though peasants, they had the blood of kings in their veins, and belonged to the ancient and royal town of Bethlehem, in the far south of the country. Day by day the edict, like an invisible hand, forced them southward along the weary road, until at last they climbed the rocky ascent that led to the gate of the town—he terrified with anxiety, and she well-nigh dead with fatigue. They reached the inn, but found it crowded with strangers who, there on the same errand as themselves, had arrived before them. No friendly house opened its door to receive them, so they had to clear for their lodging a corner of the innyard, occupied also by the beasts of the numerous travelers. There, that very night, she brought forth her first-born Son; and, because there was neither womanly hand to assist her nor bed to receive Him, she wrapped Him in swaddling clothes and laid Him in a manger.

3. Such was the manner of the birth of Jesus. I never felt the full pathos of the scene until, standing one day in a room of an old inn in the market town of Eisleben, in Central Germany, I was told that on that very spot, four centuries earlier, amidst the noise of a market day and the bustle of a public house, the wife of the poor miner, Hans Luther, who happened to be in town on business, being surprised like Mary with sudden birth pangs, brought

forth in sorrow and poverty the child who was to become Martin Luther, the hero of the Reformation and the designer of modern Europe.

4. The next morning the noise and bustle broke out again in the inn and innyard; the citizens of Bethlehem went about their work; the registration proceeded; but during that time the greatest event in the history of the world had taken place. We never know where a great beginning may be happening. Every arrival of a new soul in the world is a mystery and a closed box of possibilities. Joseph and Mary alone knew the tremendous secret—that on her, the peasant maiden and carpenter's bride, had been conferred the honor of being the mother of Him who was the Messiah of her race, the Savior of the world, and the Son of God.

5. It had been foretold in ancient prophecy that He would be born on this very spot: "But thou, Bethlehem Ephratah, though thou be little among the thousands of Judah, yet out of thee shall he come forth unto me that is to be ruler in Israel." The proud emperor's decree drove the anxious couple southward. Yes, but another hand was leading them on—the hand of Him who overrules the purposes of emperors and kings, of statesmen and parliaments, for the accomplishment of His designs, though they know them not; who hardened the heart of Pharaoh, called Cyrus like a slave to His foot, made the mighty Nebuchadnezzar His servant, and in the same way could overrule for His own far-reaching purposes the pride and ambition of Augustus.

THE GROUP AROUND THE INFANT

6. Although Jesus made His entry on the stage of life so humbly and silently; although the citizens of

Bethlehem did not dream what had happened in their midst; although the emperor at Rome did not know that his decree had influenced the nativity of a King who was yet to bear rule, not only over the Roman world, but over many a land where Rome's eagles never flew; although the history of mankind went thundering forward the next morning in the channels of its ordinary interests, quite unconscious of the event that had happened, yet it did not altogether escape notice. As the babe leaped in the womb of the aged Elizabeth when the mother of her Lord approached her, so, when He who brought the new world with Him appeared, there sprang up anticipations and forebodings of the truth in various representatives of the old world that was passing away. There went through sensitive and waiting souls, here and there, a dim and half-conscious thrill, which drew them around the Infant's cradle. Look at the group that gathered to gaze on Him! It represented in miniature the whole of His future history.

7. The Shepherds. First came the shepherds from the neighboring fields. That which was unnoticed by the kings and important persons of this world was so absorbing a theme to the princes of heaven that they burst the bounds of the invisibility in which they shrouded themselves, in order to express their joy and explain the significance of the great event. And, seeking the most worthy hearts to which they might communicate it, they found them in these simple shepherds, living the life of contemplation and prayer in the suggestive fields where Jacob had kept his flocks, where Boaz and Ruth had been married, and where David, the great Old Testament type, had spent his youth. There, by the study of the secrets and needs of their own hearts, they learned far more of the nature of the Savior who was to come than the Pharisee amidst the religious pomp of the temple or the scribe burrowing without the seeing eye among the prophecies of the Old Testament. The angel directed them where the Savior was, and they hastened to the town to find Him. They were the representatives of the peasant people, with the "honest and good heart," who afterward formed the bulk of His disciples.

8. Simeon and Anna. Next to them came Simeon and Anna, the representatives of the devout and intelligent students of the Scriptures, who at that time were expecting the appearance of the Messiah and afterward contributed some of His most faithful followers. On the eighth day after His birth, the Child was circumcised, thus being "made under the law," entering into the covenant, and inscribing His name in His own blood in the roll of the nation. Soon thereafter, when the days of Mary's purification were ended, they carried Him from Bethlehem to Jerusalem to present Him to the Lord in the temple. It was "the Lord of the temple entering the temple of the Lord"; but few visitors to the spot could have been less noticed by the priests, for Mary, instead of offering the sacrifice usual in such cases, could only afford two turtle doves, the offering of the poor. Yet there were eyes looking on, undazzled by the shows and glitter of the world, from which His poverty could not conceal Him. Simeon, an aged saint, who in answer to many prayers had received a secret promise that he would not die until he had seen the Messiah, met the parents and the child. Suddenly it shot through him like a flash of lightning that this at last was He, and, taking Him up in his arms, he praised God for the advent of the Light to lighten the Gentiles and the Glory of His people Israel. While he was still speaking, another witness joined the group. It was Anna, a saintly widow, who literally dwelled in the courts of the Lord, and had purified the eye of her spirit with the practice of prayer and fasting, until it could pierce with prophetic glance the veils of sense. She united her testimony to the old man's, praising God and confirming the mighty secret to the other expectant souls who were looking for redemption in Israel.

9. The Wise Men. The shepherds and these aged saints were near the spot where the new force entered the world. But it thrilled susceptible souls at a much greater distance. It was probably after the presentation in the temple and after the parents had carried their child back to Bethlehem, where it was their intention to reside instead of returning to Nazareth, that He was visited by the Wise Men from the East. These were members of the learned class of the Magians, the repositories of science, philosophy, medical skill and religious mysteries in the countries beyond the Euphrates. Tacitus, Suetonius and Josephus tell us that in the regions from where they came there prevailed at that time an expectation that a great king was about to arise in Judaea. We know also from the calculations of the great astronomer Kepler, that at this very time there was visible in the heavens a brilliant temporary star. Now the Magi were ardent students of astrology and believed that any unusual phenomenon in the heavens was the sign of some remarkable event on earth; and it is possible that, connecting this star, to which their attention would undoubtedly be eagerly directed, with the expectation mentioned by the ancient historians, they were led westward to see if it had been fulfilled. But there must also have been awakened in them a deeper want, to which God responded. If their search began in scientific curiosity and speculation, God led it on to the perfect truth. That is His way always. Instead of making tirades against the imperfect, He speaks to us in the language we understand, even if it expresses His meaning very imperfectly, and guides us by it to the perfect truth. Just as He used astrology to lead the world to astronomy, and alchemy to bring it to chemistry, and as the Revival of Learning preceded the Reformation, so He used the knowledge of these men, which was half falsehood and superstition, to lead them to the Light of the world. Their visit was a prophecy of how in the future the gentile world would hail His doctrine and salvation, and bring its wealth and talents, its science and philosophy, to offer at His feet.

10. Herod. All these gathered around His cradle to worship the Holy Child—the shepherds in their simple wonder, Simeon and Anna with a reverence enriched by the treasured wisdom and piety of centuries, and the Magi with the lavish gifts of the Orient and the open brow of gentile knowledge. But while these worthy worshipers were gazing down on Him, a sinister and murderous face came and looked over their shoulders. It was the face of Herod. This prince then occupied the throne of the country—the throne of David and the Maccabees. But he was an alien and low-born usurper. His subjects hated him, and it was only by Roman favor that he was maintained in his seat. He was able, ambitious, and magnificent. Yet he had such a cruel, crafty, gloomy, and filthy mind, which you would find among many Oriental tyrants. He had been guilty of every crime. He had made his palace swim in blood, having murdered his own favorite wife, three of his sons, and many of his relatives. He was now old and tortured with disease, remorse, the sense of unpopularity, and a cruel terror of every possible aspirant to the throne that he had usurped. The Magi had naturally turned their steps to the capital, to inquire where He whose sign they had seen in the East, was to be born. The suggestion touched Herod in his sorest spot; but with diabolical hypocrisy he concealed his suspicions. Having learned from the priests that the Messiah was to be born in Bethlehem, he directed the strangers there, but ar-

ranged that they should return and tell him the very house
where the new King was. He hoped to cut Him off at a
single blow. But he was fooled; for, being warned by
God, the Magi did not come back to tell him, but returned
to their own country another way. Then his fury burst
forth like a storm, and he sent his soldiers to murder every
babe under two years of age in Bethlehem. He might as
well have attempted to cut a mountain of rock in two as to
cut the chain of the divine purposes. "He thrust his sword
into the nest, but the bird was flown." Joseph fled with
the child to Egypt and remained there until Herod died,
when he returned and lived at Nazareth; because had he
returned to Bethlehem, he would have been in the kingdom of Archelaus, the like-minded son of his bloodthirsty
father. Herod's murderous face, glaring down on the infant, was a sad prophecy of how the powers of the world
would persecute Him and cut off His life from the earth.

THE SILENT YEARS AT NAZARETH

11. The records that we possess up to this point are,
as we have seen, comparatively full. Our information
comes to a sudden stop with the settlement at Nazareth,
after the return from Egypt. And over the rest of the life of
Jesus, until His public ministry begins, a thick covering is
drawn, which is only lifted once. We may wish the narrative would have continued with the same fullness through
the years of His boyhood and youth. In modern biog-
raphies there are few parts more interesting than the
anecdotes that they furnish of the childhood of their subjects, for in these we can often see, in miniature and in
charming simplicity, the character and the plan of the
future life. What would we not give to know the habits,
the friendships, the thoughts, the words, and the actions
of Jesus during so many years? Only one flower of anec-
dote has been thrown over the wall of the hidden garden,

and it is so exquisite as to fill us with intense longing to see the garden itself. But it has pleased God, whose silence is no less wonderful than His words, to keep it closed.

12. It was natural that, where God was silent and curiosity was strong, the fancy of man should attempt to fill up the empty spaces. Accordingly, in the early church *Apocryphal Gospels* appeared, which pretended to give full details where the inspired Gospels were silent. They are particularly full of the sayings and doings of the childhood of Jesus. But they only show how unequal the human imagination was to such a theme, and bring out by the contrast of glitter and caricature the solidity and truthfulness of the Scripture narrative. They make Him a worker of frivolous and useless marvels, who molded birds of clay and made them fly, changed His playmates into goats, and so forth. In short, they are compilations of worthless and often blasphemous fables.

13. These grotesque failures warn us not to intrude with the suggestions of fancy into the hallowed enclosure. It is enough to know that He grew in wisdom and stature, and in favor with God and man. He was a real child and youth, and passed through all the stages of a natural development. Body and mind grew together, the one expanding to manly vigor, and the other acquiring more and more knowledge and power. His opening character exhibited a grace that made every one who saw it wonder at and love its goodness and purity.

14. But, though we are forbidden to let our fancy loose here, we are not prohibited. On the contrary, it is our duty to make use of such authentic materials as are supplied by the manners and customs of the time, or by incidents of His later life that refer back to His earlier

years, in order to connect the infancy with the period
when the narrative of the Gospels again takes up the
thread of biography. It is possible in this way to gain, at
least in some degree, a true conception of what He was as
a boy and a young man, and the influences by which His
development proceeded through so many silent years.

15. We know in what kind of home influences He
was brought up. His home was one of those which were
the glory of His country, as they are of our own—the
places of the godly and intelligent working class. Joseph,
its head, was a man saintly and wise; but the fact that he
is not mentioned in Christ's later life has generally been
believed to indicate that he died during Jesus' youth,
perhaps leaving the care of the household on His shoulders. His mother probably exercised the most decisive of
all external influences on His development. What she was
may be inferred from the fact that she was chosen from all
the women of the world to be crowned with the supreme
honor of womanhood. The song that she poured forth on
the subject of her own great destiny shows her to have
been a woman religious, fervently poetical and patriotic; a
student of Scripture, and especially of its great women,
for her song is saturated with Old Testament ideas, and
molded on Hannah's song; a spirit exquisitely humble,
yet capable of thoroughly appreciating the honor conferred on her. She was no miraculous queen of heaven, as
superstition has caricatured her, but a woman exquisitely
pure, saintly, loving and with a beautiful soul. This is
aureole enough. Jesus grew up in her love and passion-
ately returned it.

16. There were other members of the household.
Jesus had brothers and sisters. From two of them, James
and Jude, we have epistles in Holy Scripture, in which we
may read what their character was. Perhaps it is not ir-

reverent to infer from the severe tone of their epistles that, in their unbelieving state, they may have been somewhat harsh and unsympathetic men. They did not believe on Him during His lifetime, and it is not likely that they were close companions to Him in Nazareth. He was probably alone much; and the pathos of His saying, that a prophet is not without honor save in his own country and in his own house, probably reached back into the years before His ministry began.

17. He received His education at home, or from a scribe attached to the village synagogue. However, it was only a poor man's education. As the scribes contemptuously said, He had never learned, or, as we should say, He was not college educated. No; but the love of knowledge was awake in Him early. He daily knew the joy of deep and happy thought; He had the best of all keys to knowledge—the open mind and the loving heart; and the three great books lay ever open before Him—the Bible, Man and Nature.

18. It is easy to understand with what fervent enthusiasm He would devote Himself to the Old Testament; and His sayings, which are full of quotations from it, afford abundant proof of how constantly it formed the food of His mind and the comfort of His soul. His youthful study of it was the secret of the marvelous facility with which He made use of it afterward in order to enrich His preaching and enforce His doctrine, to repel the assaults of opponents, and overcome the temptations of the Evil One. His quotations also show that He read it in the original Hebrew, and not in the Greek translation, which was then in general use. The Hebrew was a dead language even in Palestine, just as Latin now is in many countries, but He would naturally long to read it in the words in which it was written. Those who have not enjoyed a lib-

eral education, but who amid many difficulties have
mastered Greek in order to read their New Testament in
the original, will perhaps best understand how, in a
country village, He made Himself master of the ancient
tongue, and with what delight He pored over the sacred
page in the rolls of the synagogue or in such manuscripts
as He may have Himself possessed. The language in
which He thought and spoke familiarly was Aramaic, a
branch of the same stem to which the Hebrew belongs.
We have fragments of it in some recorded sayings of His,
such as "Talitha, cumi," and "Eloi, Eloi lama
sabachthani." He would have the same chance of learning
Greek as a boy born in the Scottish Highlands has of
learning English, "Galilee of the Gentiles" being then full
of Greek-speaking inhabitants. Thus He was probably
master of three languages—one of them the grand religious language of the world, in whose literature He was
deeply versed; another the most perfect means of expressing secular thought that has ever existed, although there
is no evidence that He had any acquaintance with the
masterpieces of Greek literature; and the third the language of the common people, to whom His preaching was
to be especially addressed.

19. There are few places where human nature can be
better studied than in a country village; for there one sees
the whole of each individual life and knows all one's
neighbors thoroughly. In a city far more people are seen,
but far fewer known; it is only the outside of life that is
visible. In a village the view outward is circumscribed;
but the view downward is deep, and the view upward
unimpeded. Nazareth was a notoriously wicked town, as
we learn from the proverbial question, "Can any good
thing come out of Nazareth?" Jesus had no acquaintance
with sin in His own soul, but in the town He had a full
exhibition of the awful problem with which it was to be

His life work to deal. He was still further brought into contact with human nature by His trade. That He worked as a carpenter in Joseph's shop there can be no doubt. Who could know better than His own townsmen, who asked, in their astonishment at His preaching, "Is not this the carpenter?" It would be difficult to exhaust the significance of the fact that God chose for His Son, when He dwelt among men, out of all the possible positions in which He might have placed Him, the lot of a working man. It stamped men's common toils with everlasting honor. It acquainted Jesus with the feelings of the multitude, and helped Him to know what was in man. It was afterward said that He knew this so well that He did not need any man to teach Him.

20. Travelers tell us that the spot where He grew up is one of the most beautiful on the face of the earth. Nazareth is situated in a secluded, cup-like valley amid the mountains of Zebulon, just where they dip down into the plain of Esdraelon, with which it is connected by a steep and rocky path. Its white houses, with vines clinging to their walls, are embowered amidst gardens and groves of olive, fig, orange, and pomegranate trees. The fields are divided by hedges of cactus, and enameled with innumerable flowers of every hue. Behind the village rises a hill five hundred feet in height, from whose summit there is seen one of the most wonderful views in the world—the mountains of Galilee, with snowy Hermon towering above them, to the north; the ridge of Carmel, the coast of Tyre and the sparkling waters of the Mediterranean, to the west; a few miles to the east, the wooded, cone-like bulk of Tabor; and to the south, the plain of Esdraelon, with the mountains of Ephraim beyond. The preaching of Jesus shows how deeply He had drunk into the essence of natural beauty and reveled in the changing aspects of the seasons. It was when wandering as a lad in

these fields that He gathered the images of beauty that He poured out in His parables and addresses. It was on that hill that He acquired the habit later in life of retreating to the mountaintops to spend the night in solitary prayer. The doctrines of His preaching were not thought out on the spur of the moment. They were poured out in a living stream when the occasion came, but the water had been gathering into the hidden well many years before. In the fields and on the mountainside He had thought them out during the years of happy and undisturbed meditation and prayer.

21. There is still one important educational influence to be mentioned. Every year, after He was twelve years old, He went with His parents to the Passover at Jerusalem. Fortunately we have preserved for us an account of the first of these visits. It is the only occasion on which the veil is lifted during thirty years. Everyone who can remember his own first journey from a village home to the capital of his country will understand the joy and excitement with which Jesus set out. He traveled over eighty miles of a country where nearly every mile teemed with historical and inspiring memories. He mingled with the constantly growing caravan of pilgrims, who were filled with the religious enthusiasm of the great ecclesiastical event of the year. His destination was a city that was loved by every Jewish heart with a strength of affection that has never been given to any other capital—a city full of objects and memories to touch the deepest springs of interest and emotion in His breast. It was swarming at Passover time with strangers from half-a-hundred countries, speaking as many languages and wearing as many different costumes. He went to take part for the first time in an ancient solemnity suggestive of countless patriotic and sacred memories. It was no wonder that, when the day came to return home, He was so excited with the new objects of interest, that He failed to join His party at the appointed place and time. One spot above all fascinated His interest. It was the temple and especially the school there in which the masters of wisdom taught. His mind was teeming with questions which these doctors might be asked to answer. His thirst for knowledge had an opportunity for the first time to drink its fill. So it was there His anxious parents who, missing Him after a day's journey northward, returned in anxiety to seek Him, found Him, listening with excited looks to the oracles of the wisdom of the day. His answer to the reproachful question of His mother lays bare his childhood's mind, and for a moment affords a wide glance over the thoughts that used to engross Him in the fields of Nazareth. It shows that already, though so young, He had risen above the great mass of men, who drift on through life without once inquiring what may be its meaning and its end. He was aware that He had a God-appointed life work to do, which was the one purpose of His existence to accomplish. It was the passionate thought of all His life to come. It ought to be the first and last thought of every life. It recurred again and again in His later sayings, and pealed itself finally forth in the word with which He closed His career—"It is finished!"

22. It has often been asked whether Jesus knew all along that He was the Messiah, and, if not, when and how the knowledge dawned on Him—whether it was suggested by hearing from His mother the story of His birth or announced to Him from within. Did it dawn on Him all at once, or gradually? When did the plan of His career, which He carried out so unhesitatingly from the beginning of His ministry, shape itself in His mind? Was it the slow result of years of reflection, or did it come to Him at once? These questions have occupied the greatest Christian minds and received various answers. I will not

venture to answer them, and especially with His reply to
His mother before me, I cannot trust myself even to think
of a time when He did not know what His work in this
world was to be.

23. His subsequent visits to Jerusalem must have
greatly influenced the development of His mind. If He
often went back to hear and question the rabbis in the
temple schools, He must soon have discovered how shallow was their far-famed learning. It was probably on
these annual visits that He discovered the utter corruption
of the religion of the day and the need of a radical reform
of both doctrine and practice, and marked the practices
and persons that He was later to assail with the vehe-
mence of His holy indignation.

24. Such were the external conditions amidst which
the manhood of Jesus waxed toward maturity. It would be
easy to exaggerate the influence that they may be supposed to have exerted on His development. The greater
and more original a character is, the less dependent it is
on the peculiarities of its environment. It is fed from deep
well-springs within itself, and in its germ there is a type
enclosed that expands in obedience to its own laws and
bids defiance to circumstances. In any other circumstances, Jesus would doubtless have grown to be in
every important respect the same person He became in
Nazareth.

2

THE NATION
AND THE TIME

Paragraphs 25–39.

25. We now approach the time when, after thirty years of silence and obscurity in Nazareth, Jesus was to step forth on the public stage. This is therefore the place at which to take a survey of the circumstances of the nation in whose midst His work was to be done, and also to form a clear conception of His character and aims. Every great biography is the record of the entrance into the world of a new force, bringing with it something different from all that was there before, and of the way in which it gradually gets itself incorporated with the old, so as to become a part of the future. Obviously, therefore, two things are needed by those who wish to understand it—first, a clear comprehension of the nature of the new force itself; and second, a view of the world with which it is to be incorporated. Without the latter the specific difference of the former cannot be understood, nor can the manner of its reception be appreciated—the welcome with which it is received, or the opposition with which it has to struggle.

23

Jesus brought with Him into the world more that was
original and destined to modify the future history of
mankind than anyone else who has ever entered it. But
we can neither understand Him nor the fortunes that He
encountered in seeking to incorporate with history the
gift He brought, without a clear view of the condition of
the sphere within which His life was to be passed.

26. When, having finished the last chapter of the Old
Testament, we turn over the leaf and see the first chapter
of the New, we are apt to think that in Matthew we are
still among the same people and the same state of things
as we have left in Malachi. But no idea could be more
erroneous. Four centuries elapsed between Malachi and
Matthew, and brought as total a change in Palestine as a
period of the same length has almost ever brought in any
country. The very language of the people had been
changed, and customs, ideas, parties and institutions had
come into existence that would almost have prevented
Malachi, if he had risen from the dead, from recognizing
his country.

27. Politically the nation had passed through extraordinary vicissitudes. After the Exile it had been organized as a kind of sacred state under its high priests;
but conqueror after conqueror had since marched over it,
changing everything; the old hereditary monarchy had
been restored for a time by the brave Maccabees; the bat-
tle of freedom had many times been won and lost; a
usurper had sat on the throne of David; and now at last
the country was completely under the mighty Roman
power, which had extended its sway over the whole
civilized world. It was divided into several small portions,
which the foreigner held under different tenures. Galilee
and Peraea were ruled by petty kings, sons of that Herod
under whom Jesus was born, who occupied a relation to

the Roman emperor similar to that which the subject Indian kings hold to our Queen; and Judaea was under the charge of a Roman official, a subordinate of the governor of the Roman province of Syria. Roman soldiers paraded the streets of Jerusalem; Roman standards waved over the fortified places of the country; Roman tax collectors sat at the gate of every town. To the Sanhedrin, the supreme Jewish organ of government, only a shadow of power was still conceded, its presidents, the high priests, being mere puppets of Rome, set up and put down with the utmost caprice. So low had the proud nation fallen, whose ideal had always been to rule the world, and whose patriotism was a religious and national passion as intense and unquenchable as ever burned in any country.

28. In religion the changes had been equally great, and the fall equally low. In external appearance, indeed, it might have seemed as if progress had been made instead of retrogression. The nation was far more orthodox than it had been during many earlier periods of its history. Once its chief danger had been idolatry; but the chastisement of the Exile had corrected that tendency forever, and from that day on the Jews, wherever they might be living, were uncompromising monotheists. The priestly orders and offices had been thoroughly reorganized after the return from Babylon, and the temple services and annual feasts continued to be observed at Jerusalem with strict regularity. Besides, a new and most important religious institution had arisen, which almost threw the temple with its priesthood into the background. This was the synagogue with its rabbis. It does not seem to have existed in ancient times, but was called into existence after the Exile by reverence for the written Word. Synagogues were multiplied wherever Jews lived; every Sabbath they were filled with praying congregations; exhortations were delivered by the rabbis—a new order created by the need of expound-

ers to translate from the Hebrew, which had become a dead language; and nearly the whole Old Testament was read over once a year in the hearing of the people. Schools of theology, similar to our divinity schools, had sprung up, in which the rabbis were trained and the sacred books interpreted.

29. But, in spite of all this religiosity, religion had sadly declined. The externals had been multiplied, but the inner spirit had disappeared. However rude and sinful the old nation had sometimes been, it was capable in its worst periods of producing majestic religious figures, who kept high the ideal of life and preserved the connection of the nation with heaven; and the inspired voices of the prophets kept the stream of truth running fresh and clean. But during four hundred years no prophet's voice had been heard. The records of the old prophetic utterances were still preserved with almost idolatrous reverence, but there were not men with even the necessary amount of the Spirit's inspiration to understand what He had formerly written.

30. The representative religious men of the time were the Pharisees. As their name indicates, they originally arose as champions of the separateness of the Jews from other nations. This was a noble idea, so long as the distinction emphasized was holiness. But it is far more difficult to maintain this distinction than such external differences as peculiarities of dress, food, and language. These were in course of time substituted for it. The Pharisees were ardent patriots, ever willing to lay down their lives for the independence of their country, and hating the foreign yoke with impassioned bitterness. They despised and hated other races, and clung with undying faith to the hope of a glorious future for their nation. But they had so long harped on this idea, that they had come to believe themselves the special favorites of heaven, simply because they were descendants of Abraham, and had lost sight of the importance of personal character. They multiplied their Jewish peculiarities, but substituted external observances, such as fasts, prayers, tithes, washings, and sacrifices, for the important distinctions of love to God and love to man.

31. To the Pharisaic party belonged most of the scribes. They were so-called because they were both the interpreters and copyists of the Scriptures and the lawyers of the people; for, the Jewish legal code being incorporated in the Holy Scriptures, jurisprudence became a branch of theology. They were the chief interpreters in the synagogues, although any male worshiper was permitted to speak if he chose. They professed unbounded reverence for the Scriptures, counting every word and letter in them. They had a splendid opportunity of diffusing the religious principles of the Old Testament among the people, exhibiting the glorious examples of its heroes and sowing abroad the words of the prophets; for the synagogue was one of the most potent engines of instruction ever devised by any people. But they entirely missed their opportunity. They became a dry ecclesiastical and scholastic class, using their position for selfish aggrandizement, and scorning those to whom they gave stones for bread as a vulgar and unlettered riffraff. Whatever was most spiritual, living, human, and important in the Scriptures they passed by. The commentaries of their famous men multiplied generation after generation, and the pupils studied the commentaries instead of the text. Moreover, it was a rule with them that the correct interpretation of a passage was as authoritative as the text itself; and, the interpretations of the famous masters being as a matter of course believed to be correct, the mass of opinions that were held to be as precious as the

Bible itself grew to enormous proportions. These were
"the traditions of the elders." By degrees an arbitrary
system of exegesis came into vogue, by which almost any
opinion whatever could be connected with some text and
stamped with divine authority. Every new invention of
Pharisaic peculiarities was sanctioned in this way. These
were multiplied until they regulated every detail of
life—personal, domestic, social, and public. They became
so numerous, that it required a lifetime to learn them all;
and the learning of a scribe consisted in acquaintance
with them, and with the dicta of the great rabbis and the
forms of exegesis by which they were sanctioned. This
was the chaff with which they fed the people in the
synagogues. The conscience was burdened with innumerable details, every one of which was represented to be
as divinely sanctioned as any of the Ten Commandments.
This was the intolerable burden that Peter said neither he
nor his fathers had been able to bear. This was the horrible nightmare that sat so long on Paul's conscience. But
worse consequences flowed from it. It is a well-known
principle in history, that, whenever the ceremonial is elevated to the same rank with the moral, the latter will soon
be lost sight of. The scribes and Pharisees had learned
how by arbitrary exegesis and casuistical discussion to
explain away the weightiest moral obligations, and make
up for the neglect of them by multiplying ritual observances. Thus men were able to flaunt in the pride of sanc-
tity while indulging their selfishness and vile passions.
Society was rotten with vice within, and veneered over
with a self-deceptive religiosity without.

32. There was a party of protest. The Sadducees im-
pugned the authority attached to the traditions of the
fathers, demanding a return to the Bible and nothing but
the Bible, and cried out for morality in place of ritual. But
their protest was prompted merely by the spirit of denial,

and not by a warm opposite principle of religion. They were sceptical, cold-hearted, worldly men. Though they praised morality, it was a morality unwarmed and unilluminated by any contact with that upper region of divine forces from which the inspiration of the highest morality must always come. They refused to burden their consciences with the painful details of the Pharisees; but it was because they wished to live the life of comfort and self-indulgence. They ridiculed the Pharisaic exclusiveness, but had let go what was most peculiar in the character, the faith, and the hopes of their nation. They mingled freely with the Gentiles, affected Greek culture, enjoyed foreign amusements, and thought it useless to fight for the freedom of their country. An extreme section of them were the Herodians, who had given in to the usurpation of Herod and with courtly flattery attached themselves to the favor of his sons.

33. The Sadducees belonged chiefly to the upper and wealthy classes. The Pharisees and scribes formed what we should call the middle class, although also deriving many members from the higher ranks of life. The lower classes and the country people were separated by a great gulf from their wealthy neighbors, but attached themselves by admiration to the Pharisees, as the uneducated always do to the party of warmth. Below all these was a large class of those who had lost all connection with religion and well-ordered social life—the publicans, harlots, and sinners, for whose souls no man cared.

34. Such were the pitiable features of the society on which Jesus was about to discharge His influence—a nation enslaved; the upper classes devoted themselves to selfishness, courtiership, and scepticism; the teachers and chief professors of religion were lost in mere shows of ceremonialism, and boasted themselves the favorites of

God, while their souls were honeycombed with self-deception and vice; the body of the people were misled by false ideals; and, seething at the bottom of society, were a neglected mass of unblushing and unrestrained sin.

35. And this was the people of God! Yes; in spite of their awful degradation, these were the children of Abraham, Isaac, and Jacob, and the heirs of the covenant and the promises. Back beyond the centuries of degradation towered the figures of the patriarchs, the kings after God's own heart, the psalmists, the prophets, the generations of faith and hope. And in front there was greatness too! The word of God, once sent forth from heaven and uttered by the mouths of His prophets, could not return to Him void. He had said that to this nation was to be given the perfect revelation of Himself, that in it was to appear the perfect ideal of manhood, and that from it was to issue forth the regeneration of all mankind. Therefore a wonderful future still belonged to it. The river of Jewish history was for the time choked and lost in the sands of the desert, but it was destined to reappear again and flow forward on its God-appointed course. The time of fulfillment was at hand, much as the signs of the times might seem to forbid the hope. Had not all the prophets from Moses onward spoken of a great One to come, who, appearing just when the darkness was blackest and the degradation deepest, was to bring back the lost glory of the past?

36. Many faithful souls asked themselves this in the weary and degraded time. There are good men in the worst of periods. There were good men even in the selfish and corrupt Jewish parties. But especially does piety linger in such epochs in the lowly homes of the people; and, just as we are permitted to hope that at the present time there may be those who, through all the ceremonies put between the soul and Christ, reach forth to Him and by the selection of a spiritual instinct seize the truth and pass the falsehood by, so among the common people of Palestine there were those who, hearing the Scriptures read in the synagogues and reading them in their homes, instinctively neglected the cumbrous and endless comments of their teachers, and saw the glory of the past, of holiness and of God, which the scribes failed to see.

37. It was especially to the promises of a Deliverer that such spirits attached their interest. Feeling bitterly the shame of national slavery, the hollowness of the times, and the awful wickedness that rotted under the surface of society, they longed and prayed for the advent of the coming One and the restoration of the national character and glory.

38. The scribes also busied themselves with this element in the Scriptures; and the cherishing of messianic hopes was one of the chief distinctions of the Pharisees. But they had caricatured the prophetic utterances on the subject by their arbitrary interpretations, and painted the future in colors borrowed from their own carnal imaginations. They spoke of the advent as the coming of the kingdom of God, and of the Messiah as the Son of God. But what they chiefly expected Him to do was, by the working of marvels and by irresistible force, to free the nation from servitude and raise it to the utmost worldly grandeur. They entertained no doubt that, simply because they were members of the chosen nation, they would be allotted high places in the kingdom, and never suspected that any change was needed in themselves to meet Him. The spiritual elements of the better time, holiness and love, were lost in their minds behind the dazzling forms of material glory.

39. Such was the aspect of Jewish history at the time when the hour of realizing the national destiny was about

to strike. It imparted to the work that lay before the Messiah a peculiar complexity. It might have been expected that He would find a nation saturated with the ideas and inspired with the visions of His predecessors, the prophets, at whose head He might place Himself, and from which He might receive an enthusiastic and effective cooperation. But it was not so. He appeared at a time when the nation had lapsed from its ideals and caricatured their sublimest features. Instead of meeting a nation mature in holiness and consecrated to the heaven-ordained task of blessing all other peoples, which He might easily lead up to its own final development, and then lead forth to the spiritual conquest of the world, He found that the first work that lay before Him was to proclaim a reformation in His own country, and encounter the opposition of prejudices that had accumulated there through centuries of degradation.

3

THE FINAL STAGES
OF HIS PREPARATION

Paragraphs 30–55.

40. Meanwhile He, whom so many in their own ways were hoping for, was in the midst of them, though they did not suspect it. Little could they think that He about whom they were speculating and praying was growing up in a carpenter's home in despised Nazareth. Yet so He was. There He was preparing Himself for His career. His mind was busy grasping the vast proportions of the task before Him, as the prophecies of the past and the facts of the case determined it; His eyes were looking forth on the country, and His heart was smarting with the sense of its sin and shame. In Himself He felt the gigantic powers necessary to cope with the vast design moving; and the desire to go forth and utter the thought within Him, and do the work that had been given Him to do was gradually growing to an irresistible passion.

41. Jesus had only three years to accomplish His life work. If we remember how quickly three years in an ordinary life pass away and how little at their close there usually is to show for them, we shall see what must have been the size and quality of that character, and the unity and intensity of design in that life which in so marvelously short a time made such a deep and ineffaceable impression on the world and left to mankind such a heritage of truth and influence.

42. It is generally allowed that Jesus appeared as a public man with a mind whose ideas were completely developed and arranged, with a character sharpened over its whole surface into perfect definiteness, and with designs that marched forward to their ends without hesitation. No deflection took place during the three years from the lines on which at the beginning of them He was moving. The reason of this must have been that, during the thirty years before His public work began, His ideas, His character and designs went through all the stages of a thorough development. Unpretentious as the external aspects of His life at Nazareth were, it was, below the surface, a life of intensity, variety, and grandeur. Beneath its silence and obscurity there went on all the processes of growth that issued in the magnificent flower and fruit to which all ages now look back with wonder. His preparation lasted long. For one with His powers at command, thirty years of complete reticence and reserve were a long time. Nothing was greater in Him afterward than the majestic reserve in both speech and action that characterized Him. This, too, was learned in Nazareth. There He waited until the hour of the completion of His preparation struck. Nothing could tempt Him forth before the time—not the burning desire to interfere with indignant protest amid the crying corruptions and mistakes of the age, not even the swellings of the passion to do His fellowmen good.

43. At last, however, He threw down the carpenter's tools, laid aside the workman's dress, and bade His home and the beloved valley of Nazareth farewell. Still, however, all was not ready. His manhood, though it had grown in secret to such noble proportions, still required a peculiar endowment for the work He had to do; and His ideas and designs, mature as they were, needed to be hardened in the fire of a momentous trial. The two final incidents of His preparation—the Baptism and the Temptation—still had to take place.

HIS BAPTISM

44. Jesus did not descend on the nation from the obscurity of Nazareth without note of warning. His work may be said to have been begun before He put His hand to it.

45. Once more, before hearing the voice of its Messiah, the nation was to hear the long silent voice of prophecy. The news went through all the country that in the desert of Judaea a preacher had appeared—not like the mumblers of dead men's ideas who spoke in the synagogues, or the courtier-like, smooth-tongued teachers of Jerusalem, but a rude, strong man, speaking from the heart to the heart, with the authority of one who was sure of his inspiration. He had been a Nazarite from the womb; he had lived for years in the desert, wandering, in communion with his own heart, beside the lonely shores of the Dead Sea; he was clad in the hairy cloak and leather girdle of the old prophets; and his ascetic rigor sought no finer fare than locusts and the wild honey he found in the wilderness. Yet he knew life well: he was acquainted with all the evils of the time, the hypocrisy of the religious parties, and the corruption of the masses; he had a wonderful power of searching the heart and shaking the conscience, and without fear laid bare the darling sins of every class. But that which most of all attracted attention to him and thrilled every Jewish heart from one end of the land to the other was the message he bore: which was nothing less than that the Messiah was just at hand, and about to set up the kingdom of God. All Jerusalem poured out to him; the Pharisees were eager to hear the messianic news; and even the Sadducees were stirred for a moment from their lethargy. The provinces sent their thousands to his preaching, and the scattered and hidden ones who longed and prayed for the redemption of Israel flocked to welcome the heartstirring promise. But along with it John had another message, which excited very different feelings in different minds. He had to tell his hearers that the nation as a whole was utterly unprepared for the Messiah; that the mere fact of their descent from Abraham would not be a sufficient token of admission to His kingdom; it was to be a kingdom of righteousness and holiness, and Christ's first work would be to reject all who were not marked with these qualities, as the farmer winnows away the chaff with his fan, and the master of the vineyard hews down every tree that does not produce fruit. Therefore he called the nation at large—every class and every individual—to repentance, so long as there still was time, as an indispensable preparation for enjoying the blessings of the new era; and, as an outward symbol of this inward change, he baptized in the Jordan all who received his message with faith. Many were stirred with fear and hope and submitted to the rite, but many more were irritated by the exposure of their sins and turned away in anger and unbelief. Among these were the Pharisees, on whom he was especially severe, and who were deeply offended because he had treated so lightly their descent from Abraham, on which they laid so much stress.

46. One day there appeared among the Baptist's hearers One who particularly attracted his attention, and made his voice, which had never faltered when accusing in the most vigorous language of reproof even the highest teachers and priests of the nation, tremble with a lack of self-confidence. And, when He presented Himself, after the discourse was done, among the candidates for baptism, John drew back, feeling that this was no subject for the bath of repentance, which without hesitation he had administered to all others. He felt he had no right to baptize Him. There was in His face a majesty, a purity and a peace that smote the man of rock with the sense of unworthiness and sin. It was Jesus, who had come straight from the workshop of Nazareth. John and Jesus appear never to have met before, though their families were related and the connection of their careers had been predicted before birth. This may have been due to the distance of their homes in Galilee and Judaea, and still more to the Baptist's unusual habits. But when, in obedience to the injunction of Jesus, John proceeded to administer the rite, he learned the meaning of the overpowering impression that the Stranger had made on him: for the sign was given by which, as God had instructed him, he was to recognize the Messiah, whose forerunner he was: the Holy Spirit descended on Jesus, as He emerged from the water in the attitude of prayer, and the voice of God pronounced Him in thunder His beloved Son.

47. The impression made on John by the look of Jesus reveals far better than many words could His aspect when He was about to begin His work, and the qualities of the character that in Nazareth had been slowly ripening to full maturity.

48. The baptism itself had an important significance for Jesus. To the other candidates who underwent the rite it had a double meaning: it signified the abandonment of their old sins and their entrance into the new messianic era. To Jesus it could not have the former meaning, except insofar as He may have identified Himself with His nation and taken this way of expressing His sense of its need of cleansing. But it meant that He too was now entering through this door into the new epoch, of which He was Himself to be the Author. It expressed His sense that the time had come to leave behind the employments of Nazareth and devote Himself to His peculiar work.

49. But still more important was the descent on Him of the Holy Spirit. This was neither a meaningless display nor merely given as a signal to the Baptist. It was the symbol of a special gift then given to qualify Him for His work, and to crown the long development of His unusual powers. It is a forgotten truth, that the manhood of Jesus was from first to last dependent on the Holy Spirit. We are apt to imagine that its connection with His divine nature rendered this unnecessary. On the contrary, it made it far more necessary, for in order to be the organ of His divine nature, His human nature had both to be endowed with the highest gifts and constantly sustained in their exercise. We are in the habit of attributing the wisdom and grace of His words, His supernatural knowledge of even the thoughts of men, and the miracles He performed, to His divine nature. But in the Gospels they are constantly attributed to the Holy Spirit. This does not mean that they were independent of His divine nature, but that in them His human nature was enabled to be the organ of His divine nature by a special gift of the Holy Spirit. This gift was given Him at His baptism. It was analogous to the possession of prophets, like Isaiah and Jeremiah, with the Spirit of inspiration on those occasions, of which they have left accounts, when they were called to begin their public life, and to the special outpouring of the same influence still sometimes given at their ordination to those who are about to begin the work of the ministry. But to Him it was given without measure, while to others it has always been given only in measure; and it comprised especially the gift of miraculous powers.

THE TEMPTATION

50. An immediate effect of this new endowment appears to have been one often experienced, in less degree, by others who, in their small measure, have received this same gift of the Spirit for work. His whole being was excited about His work, His desires to be engaged in it were raised to the highest pitch, and His thoughts were intensely occupied about the means of its accomplishment. Although His preparation for it had been going on for many years, although His whole heart had long been fixed on it, and His plan had been clearly settled, it was natural that, when the divine signal had been given that it was time to begin, and He felt Himself suddenly put in possession of the supernatural powers necessary for carrying it out, His mind should be in a tumult of crowding thoughts and feelings, and that He should seek a place of solitude to revolve once more the whole situation. Accordingly, He hastily retreated from the bank of the Jordan, driven, we are told, by the Spirit, who had just been given Him, into the wilderness, where, for forty days, He wandered among the sandy dunes and wild mountains, His mind being so highly strung with the emotions and ideas that crowded on Him, that He forgot even to eat.

51. But it is with surprise and awe we learn that His soul was, during those days, the scene of a frightful struggle. He was tempted of Satan, we are told. What could He be tempted with at a time so sacred? To understand this we must recall what has been said of the state of the Jewish nation, and especially the nature of the messianic hopes that they were entertaining. They expected a Messiah who would work dazzling wonders and establish a world-wide empire with Jerusalem as its center, and they had postponed the ideas of righteousness and holiness to these. They completely inverted the divine conception of the kingdom, which could not but give the spiritual and moral elements precedence of material and political considerations. Now what Jesus was tempted to do was, in carrying out the great work that His Father had committed to Him, to yield in some measure to these expectations. He must have foreseen that, unless He did so, the nation would be disappointed, and probably turn away from Him in unbelief and anger. The different temptations were only various modifications of this one thought. The suggestion that He should turn stones into bread to satisfy His hunger was a temptation to use the power of working miracles, with which He had just been endowed, for a purpose inferior to those for which alone it had been given. This was the precursor of such temptations later in His ministry as the demand of the multitude to show them a sign, or that He should come down from the cross, that they might believe Him. The suggestion that He should leap from the pinnacle of the temple was probably also a temptation to gratify the vulgar desire for wonders, because it was a part of the popular belief that the Messiah would appear suddenly, and in some marvelous way, as, for instance, by a leap from the temple roof into the midst of the crowds assembled below. The third and greatest temptation, to win the empire of all the kingdoms of the world by an act of worship to the Evil One, was manifestly only a symbol of obedience to the universal Jewish conception of the coming kingdom as a vast structure of material force. It was a temptation that every worker for God, weary with the slow progress of goodness, must often feel, and to which even good and earnest men have sometimes given way—to begin at the outside instead of within, to get first a great shell of external conformity to religion and afterward fill it with the reality. It was the temptation to which Mahomet yielded, when he used the sword to subdue those whom he was later to make religious, and to which the Jesuits yielded, when they baptized the heathen first and evangelized them afterward.

52. It is with awe that we think of these suggestions presenting themselves to the holy soul of Jesus. Could He be tempted to distrust God and even to worship the Evil One? No doubt the temptations were flung from Him, as the impotent billows retire broken from the breast of the rock on which they have dashed themselves. But these temptations pressed in on Him, not only at this time, but often before in the valley of Nazareth and often afterward in the heat and crises of His life. We must remember that it is no sin to be tempted, it is only sin to yield to temptation. And, indeed, the more absolutely pure a soul is, the more painful will be the point of the temptation, as it presses for admission into his breast.

53. Although the tempter only departed from Jesus for a season, this was a decisive struggle; he was thoroughly beaten back, and his power broken at its heart. Milton has indicated this by finishing his *Paradise Regained* at this point. Jesus emerged from the wilderness with the plan of His life, which, no doubt, had been formed long before, hardened in the fire of trial. Nothing is more conspicuous in His later life than the resolution with which He carried it out. Other men, even those who have accomplished the greatest tasks, have sometimes had no definite plan, but have only seen by degrees, in the evolution of circumstances, the path to pursue; their purposes have been modified by events and the advice of others. But Jesus started with His plan perfected, and never deviated from it by a hair's breadth. He resented the interference of His mother or His chief disciple with it as stedfastly as He bore it through the fiery opposition of open enemies. And His plan was to establish the kingdom of God in the hearts of individuals, and to rely not on the weapons of political and material strength, but only on the power of love and the force of truth.

THE DIVISIONS OF HIS PUBLIC MINISTRY

54. The public ministry of Jesus is generally considered to have lasted three years. Each of them had unusual features of its own. The first may be called the Year of Obscurity, both because the records of it that we possess are very scanty, and because He seems during it to have been only slowly emerging into public notice. It was spent for the most part in Judaea. The second was the Year of Public Favor, during which the country had become thoroughly aware of Him, His activity was incessant, and His fame rang through the length and breadth of the land. It was almost wholly passed in Galilee. The third was the Year of Opposition, when the public favor ebbed away, His enemies multiplied and assailed Him with more and more persistance, and at last He fell a victim to their hatred. The first six months of this final year were passed in Galilee, and the last six in other parts of the land.

55. Thus the life of the Savior in its external outline resembled that of many a reformer and benefactor of mankind. Such a life often begins with a period during which the public is gradually made aware of the new man in its midst, then passes into a period when his doctrine or reform is borne aloft on the shoulders of popularity, and finally ends with a reaction, when the old prejudices and interests that have been assailed by him rally from his attack and, gaining to themselves the passions of the crowd, crush him in their rage.

4

THE YEAR
OF OBSCURITY

56. The records of this year that we possess are ex-
tremely meager, comprising only two or three incidents,
which may be here enumerated, especially as they form a
kind of program of His future work.

57. When He emerged from the wilderness after the
forty days of temptation, with His grasp of His future plan
tightened by that awful struggle and with the inspiration
of His baptism still swelling His heart, He appeared once
more on the bank of the Jordan, and John pointed Him
out as the great Successor to himself of whom he had often
spoken. He especially introduced Him to some of the
choicest of his own disciples, who immediately became
His followers. Probably the first of these to whom He
spoke was the man who was later to be His favorite disciple and would give to the world the divinest portrait of
His character and life. John the Evangelist—for he it
was—has left an account of this first meeting and the
interview that followed it, which retains in all its freshness the impression that Christ's majesty and purity made
on his receptive mind. The other young men who at-

tached themselves to Him at the same time were Andrew, Peter, Philip, and Nathanael. They had been prepared for their new Master by their relationship with the Baptist, and, although they did not at once give up their occupations and follow Him in the same way as they did at a later period, they received impressions at their first meeting that decided their whole career. The Baptist's disciples do not seem to have at once gone over in a body to Christ. But the best of them did so. Some troublemakers endeavored to excite envy in his mind by pointing out how his influence was passing away to another. But they little understood that great man, whose chief greatness was his humility. He answered them that it was his joy to decrease, while Christ increased, for it was Christ who as the Bridegroom was to lead home the bride, while he was only the Bridegroom's friend, whose happiness consisted in seeing the crown of festal joy placed on the head of another.

58. With His newly acquired followers Jesus departed from the scene of John's ministry, and went north to Cana in Galilee, to attend a marriage to which He had been invited. Here He made the first display of the miraculous powers with which He had been recently endowed, by turning water into wine. It was a manifestation of His glory intended especially for His new disciples, who, we are told, thereafter believed on Him, which means, no doubt, that they were fully convinced that He was the Messiah. It was intended also to strike the keynote of His ministry as altogether different from the Baptist's. John was an ascetic hermit, who fled from the abodes of men and called his hearers out into the wilderness. But Jesus had glad tidings to bring to men's hearts; He was to mingle in their common life and produce a happy revolution in their circumstances, which would be like the turning.of the water of their life into wine.

59. Soon after this miracle He returned again to Judaea to attend the Passover, and gave a still more striking proof of the joyful and enthusiastic mood in which He was then living, by purging the temple of the sellers of animals and the moneychangers, who had introduced their traffic into its courts. These persons were allowed to carry on their sacrilegious trade under the pretence of accommodating strangers who came to worship at Jerusalem, by selling to them the victims that they could not bring from foreign countries, and supplying, in exchange for foreign money, the Jewish coins in which alone they could pay their temple dues. But what had been begun under the veil of a pious pretext had ended in gross disturbance of the worship, and in elbowing the gentile proselytes from the place that God had allowed them in His house. Jesus had probably often witnessed the disgraceful scene with indignation during His visits to Jerusalem, and now, with the prophetic zeal of His baptism upon Him, He lashed out against it. The same look of irresistible purity and majesty which had appalled John when He sought baptism, prevented any resistance on the part of the ignoble crew, and made the onlookers recognize the distinguishing characteristics of the prophets of ancient days, before whom kings and crowds alike were likely to tremble. It was the beginning of His reformatory work against the religious abuses of the time.

60. He performed other miracles during the feast, which must have excited much talk among the pilgrims from every land who crowded the city. One result was that a follower brought to His lodging one night the venerable and anxious inquirer to whom He delivered the marvelous discourse on the nature of the new kingdom that He had come to found, and the grounds of admission to it, which has been preserved for us in the third chapter of John. It seemed a hopeful sign that one of the heads of the nation should approach Him in a spirit so humble; but Nicodemus was the only one of them on whose mind the first display of the Messiah's power in the capital produced a deep and favorable impression.

61. Thus far we follow clearly the first steps of Jesus. But at this point our information regarding the first year of His ministry, after starting with such fullness, comes to a sudden stop, and we learn nothing more about His next eight months but that He was baptizing in Judaea—"though Jesus himself baptized not, but his disciples"—and that He "made and baptized more disciples than John."

62. What can be the meaning of such a blank? It is to be noted, too, that it is only in the fourth Gospel that we receive even the details given above. The synoptists omit the first year of the ministry altogether, beginning their narrative with the ministry in Galilee, and merely indicating in the most cursory way that there was a ministry in Judaea earlier.

63. It is very difficult to explain all this. The most natural explanation would perhaps be that the incidents of this year were imperfectly known at the time when the Gospels were written. It would be natural that the details of the period when Jesus had not yet attracted much public attention should be less accurately remembered than those of the period when He was by far the best known personage in the country. But, indeed, the synoptists all through their Gospels take little notice of what happened in Judaea, until the close of His life draws near. It is to John we are indebted for the connected narrative of His various visits to the south.

64. But John, at least, could scarcely have been ignorant of the incidents of eight months. We shall perhaps be conducted to the explanation by attending to the little-noticed fact, which John communicates, that for a time Jesus took up the work of the Baptist. He baptized by the hands of His disciples, and drew even larger crowds than John. Must not this mean that He was convinced, by the small impression that His manifestation of Himself at the Passover had made, that the nation was utterly unprepared for receiving Him yet as the Messiah, and that what was needed was the extension of the preparatory work of repentance and baptism, and accordingly, keeping in the background His higher character, became for the time the colleague of John? This view is confirmed by the fact that it was upon John's imprisonment at this year's end that He opened fully His messianic career in Galilee.

65. A still deeper explanation of the silence of the synoptists over this period, and their scant notice of Christ's subsequent visits to Jerusalem, has been suggested. Jesus came primarily to the Jewish nation, whose authoritative representatives were to be found at Jerusalem. He was the Messiah promised to their fathers, the Fulfiller of the nation's history. He had indeed a far wider mission to the whole world, but He was to begin with the Jews, and at Jerusalem. The nation, however, in its heads at Jerusalem, rejected Him, so He was compelled to found His world-wide community from a different center. This having become evident by the time the Gospels were written, the synoptists passed His activity at the headquarters of the nation, as a work with merely negative results, in great measure by, and concentrated attention on the period of His ministry when He was gathering the company of believing souls that was to form the nucleus of the Christian church. However this may be, certainly at the close of the first year of the ministry of Jesus there fell already over Judaea and Jerusalem the shadow of

5

THE YEAR
OF PUBLIC FAVOR

66. After the year spent in the south, Jesus shifted the sphere of His activity to the north of the country. In Galilee He would be able to address Himself to minds that were unsophisticated with the prejudices and supercilious pride of Judaea, where the sacerdotal and learned classes had their headquarters; and He might hope that, if His doctrine and influence took a deep hold of one part of the country, even though it was remote from the center of authority, He might return to the south backed with an irresistible national acknowledgment, and carry by storm even the citadel of prejudice itself.

GALILEE

67. The area of His activity for the next eighteen months was very limited. Even the whole of Palestine was a very limited country. Its length was a hundred miles less than that of Scotland, and its breadth considerably less than the average breadth of Scotland. It is important to remember this, because it renders intelligible the rapidity with which the movement of Jesus spread over the land, and all parts of the country flocked to His ministry. It is also interesting to remember it as an illustration of the fact that the nations that have contributed most to the civilization of the world have, during the period of their true greatness, been confined to very small territories. Rome was but a single city, and Greece a very small country.

68. Galilee was the most northerly of the four provinces into which Palestine was divided. It was sixty miles long by thirty wide. It consisted for the most part of an elevated plateau, whose surface was varied by irregular mountain masses. Near its eastern boundary it dropped down into a great gulf, through which flowed the Jordan, and in the midst of which, at a depth of five hundred feet below the Mediterranean, lay the lovely, harp-shaped Sea of Galilee. The whole province was very fertile, and its surface was thickly covered with large villages and towns. The population was perhaps as dense as that of Lancashire or the West Riding of Yorkshire. But the center of activity was the basin of the lake, a sheet of water thirteen miles long by six wide. Above its eastern shore, around which ran a fringe of green a quarter of a mile wide, there towered high, bare hills, divided with the channels of torrents. On the western side, the mountains were gently sloped and their sides richly cultivated, bearing bountiful crops of every description; while at their feet the shore was verdant with luxuriant groves of olives, oranges, figs, and every product of an almost tropical climate. At the northern end of the lake the space between the water and the mountains was broadened by the delta of the river and watered with many streams from the hills, so that it was a perfect paradise of fertility and beauty. It was called the plain of Gennesareth, and even today, when the whole basin of the lake is little better than a torrid solitude, it is still covered with magnificent cornfields, wherever the hand of cultivation touches it; and, where idleness leaves it untended, is overspread with thick jungles of thorn and oleander. In our Lord's time, it contained the chief cities on the lake, such as Capernaum, Bethsaida, and Chorazin. But the whole shore was studded with towns and villages, and formed a perfect beehive of swarming human life. The means of existence were abundant in the crops and fruits of every description which the fields yielded so richly; and the waters of the lake teemed with fish, affording employment to thousands of fishermen. Besides, the great highways from Egypt to Damascus, and from Phoenicia to the Euphrates, passed here, and made this a vast center of traffic. Thousands of boats for fishing, transport and pleasure moved to and fro on the surface of the lake, so that the whole region was a focus of energy and prosperity.

69. The report of the miracles that Jesus had performed at Jerusalem, eight months before, had been brought home to Galilee by the pilgrims who had been south at the feast, and doubtless also the news of His preaching and baptism in Judaea had created talk and excitement before He arrived. Accordingly, the Galileans were in some measure prepared to receive Him when He returned to their midst.

70. One of the first places He visited was Nazareth, the home of His childhood and youth. He appeared there one Sabbath in the synagogue, and, being now known as a preacher, was invited to read the Scriptures and address the congregation. He read a passage in Isaiah, in which a glowing description is given of the coming and work of the Messiah: "The Spirit of the Lord is upon me, because he hath anointed me to preach the gospel to the poor; he hath sent me to heal the brokenhearted, to preach deliverance to the captives, and recovering of sight to the blind, to set at liberty them that are bruised, to preach the acceptable year of the Lord." As He commented on this text, picturing the features of the messianic time—the emancipation of the slave, the enriching of the poor, the healing of the diseased—their curiosity at hearing for the first time a young preacher who had been brought up among them passed into spellbound wonder, and they burst into the applause that used to be allowed in the Jewish synagogues. But soon the reaction came. They began to whisper: Was not this the carpenter who had worked among them? Had not His father and mother been their neighbors? Were not His sisters married in the town? Their envy was excited. And when He proceeded to tell them that the prophecy that He had read was fulfilled in Himself, they broke out into angry scorn. They demanded of Him a sign, such as it was reported He had given in Jerusalem; and, when He informed them that He could do no miracle among the unbelieving, they rushed on Him in a storm of jealousy and wrath, and, hurrying Him out of the synagogue to a crag behind the town, would, if He had not miraculously taken Himself away from them, have flung Him over and crowned their proverbial wickedness with a deed that would have robbed Jerusalem of her bad eminence of being the murderess of the Messiah.

71. From that day Nazareth was His home no more. Once again, indeed, in His yearning love for His old neighbors, He visited it, but with no better result. From that point on He made His home in Capernaum, on the northwestern shore of the Sea of Galilee. This town has completely vanished out of existence; its very site cannot now be discovered with any certainty. This may be one reason why it is not connected in the Christian mind with the life of Jesus in the same prominent way as Bethlehem, where He was born, Nazareth, where He was brought up, and Jerusalem, where He died. But we ought to fix it in our memories side by side with these, for it was His home for eighteen of the most important months of His life. It is called His own city, and He was asked for tribute in it as a citizen of the place. It was thoroughly well adapted to be the center of His labors in Galilee, for it was the focus of the busy life in the basin of the lake, and was conveniently situated for excursions to all parts of the province. Whatever happened there was quickly heard of in all the regions round about.

72. In Capernaum, then, He began His Galilean work; and for many months the method of His life was—to be frequently there as in His headquarters, and from this center to make tours in all directions, visiting the towns and villages of Galilee. Sometimes His journey would be inland, to the west. At other times it would be a tour of the villages on the lake or a visit to the country on its eastern side. He had a boat that waited on Him, to convey Him wherever He might wish to go. He would come back to Capernaum, perhaps only for a day, perhaps for a week or two at a time.

73. In a few weeks the whole province was ringing with His name; He was the subject of conversation in every boat on the lake and every house in the whole region; men's minds were stirred with the profoundest excitement, and everyone desired to see Him. Crowds began to gather about Him. They grew larger and larger. They multiplied to thousands and tens of thousands. They followed Him wherever He went. The news spread far and wide beyond Galilee and brought hosts from Jerusalem, Judaea and Peraea, and even from Idumaea in the far south and Tyre and Sidon in the far north. Sometimes He could not stay in any town, because the crowds blocked up the streets and stepped on each other. He had to take them out to the fields and deserts. The country was stirred up from end to end, and Galilee was all on fire with excitement about Him.

THE MEANS HE EMPLOYED

74. How was it that He produced so great and widespread a movement? It was not by declaring Himself the Messiah. That would, indeed, have caused to pass through every Jewish breast the deepest thrill it could experience. Although Jesus now and then, as at Nazareth, revealed Himself, in general He rather concealed His true character. No doubt the reason of this was that among the excitable crowds of rude Galilee, with their grossly materialistic hopes, the declaration would have excited a revolutionary uprising against the Roman government, which would have drawn men's minds from His true aims and brought down on His head the Roman sword, just as in Judaea it would have precipitated a murderous attack on His life by the Jewish authorities. To avert either kind of interruption, He kept the full revelation of Himself in reserve, endeavoring to prepare the public mind to receive it in its true inward and spiritual meaning, when the right moment for divulging it should come, and in the meantime leaving it to be inferred from His character and work who He was.

75. The two great means that Jesus used in His work, and which created such attention and enthusiasm, were His miracles and His preaching.

THE MIRACLE-WORKER

76. Perhaps His miracles excited the widest attention. We are told how the news of the first one that He performed in Capernaum spread like wildfire through the town and brought crowds about the house where He was; and, whenever He performed a new one of extraordinary character, the excitement grew intense and the rumor of it spread on every hand. When, for instance, He first cured leprosy, the most malignant form of bodily disease in Palestine, the amazement of the people knew no bounds. It was the same when He first overcame a case of demon possession; and, when He raised to life the widow's son at Nain, there followed a sort of stupor of fear, followed by delighted wonder and the talk of thousands of tongues. All Galilee was for a time in motion with the crowding of the diseased of every description who could walk or totter to be near Him, and with companies of anxious friends carrying on beds and couches those who could not come themselves. The streets of the villages and towns were lined with the victims of disease as His gracious figure passed by. Sometimes He had so many to attend to that He could not find time even to eat; and at

one period He was so absorbed in His benevolent labors, and so carried along with the holy excitement that they caused, that His relatives, with unseemly rashness, sought to interfere, saying to each other that He was beside Himself.

77. The miracles of Jesus, taken altogether, were of two classes—those performed on man, and those performed in the sphere of external nature, such as the turning of water into wine, stilling the tempest, and multiplying the loaves. The former were by far the more numerous. They consisted chiefly of cures of diseases less or more malignant, such as lameness, blindness, deafness, palsy, and leprosy. He appears to have varied much His mode of acting, for reasons that we can scarcely explain. Sometimes He used means, such as a touch, or the laying of moistened clay on the ailing part, or ordering the patient to wash in water. At other times He healed without any means, and occasionally even at a distance. Besides these bodily cures, He dealt with the diseases of the mind. These seem to have been peculiarly prevalent in Palestine at the time and to have excited the utmost terror. They were believed to be accompanied by the entrance of demons into the poor imbecile or raving victims, and this idea was only too true. The man whom Jesus cured among the tombs in the country of the Gadarenes was a frightful example of this class of disease; and the picture of him sitting at the feet of Jesus, clothed and in his right mind, shows what an effect the kind, soothing, and authoritative presence of Jesus had on minds so distracted. But the most extraordinary of the miracles of Jesus on man were the instances in which He raised the dead to life. They were not frequent, but naturally produced an overwhelming impression whenever they occurred. The miracles of the other class—those on external nature—were of the same inexplicable description. Some of His cures of

mental disease, if standing by themselves, might be accounted for by the influence of a powerful nature on a troubled mind; and in the same way some of His bodily cures might be accounted for by His influencing the body through the mind. But such a miracle as walking on the tempestuous sea is utterly beyond the reach of any natural explanation.

78. Why did Jesus employ this means of working? Several answers may be given to this question.

79. First, He performed miracles because His Father gave Him these signs as proofs that He had sent Him. Many of the Old Testament prophets had received the same authentication of their mission, and, although John, who revived the prophetic function, worked no miracles, as the Gospels inform us with the most simple veracity, it was to be expected that He who was a far greater prophet than the greatest who went before Him should show even greater signs than any of them of His divine mission. It was a stupendous claim that He made on the faith of men when He announced Himself as the Messiah, and it would have been unreasonable to expect it to be conceded by a nation accustomed to miracles as the signs of a divine mission, if He had wrought none.

80. Second, the miracles of Christ were the natural outflow of the divine fullness that dwelled in Him. God was in Him, and His human nature was endowed with the Holy Spirit without measure. It was natural, when such a Being was in the world, that mighty works should manifest themselves in Him. He was Himself the great miracle, of which His particular miracles were merely sparks or emanations. He was the great interruption of the order of nature, or rather a new element that had entered into the order of nature to enrich and ennoble it, and His miracles entered with Him, not to disturb, but to repair its harmony. Therefore all His miracles bore the stamp of His character. They were not mere exhibitions of power, but also of holiness, wisdom, and love. The Jews often sought from Him mere gigantic wonders, to gratify their mania for marvels. But He always refused them, working only such miracles as were helps to faith. He demanded faith in all those whom He cured, and never responded either to curiosity or unbelieving challenges to exhibit marvels. This distinguishes His miracles from those fabled of ancient wonder-workers and medieval saints. His were marked by unvarying sobriety and benevolence, because they were the expressions of His character as a whole.

81. Third, His miracles were symbols of His spiritual and saving work. You have only to consider them for a moment to see that they were, as a whole, triumphs over the misery of the world. Mankind is the prey of a thousand evils, and even the frame of external nature bears the mark of some past catastrophe: "The whole creation groaneth and travaileth in pain." This huge mass of physical evil in the lot of mankind is the effect of sin. Not that every disease and misfortune can be traced to special sin, although some of them can. The consequences of past sin are distributed in detail over the whole race. But yet the misery of the world is the shadow of its sin. Material and moral evil, being thus intimately related, mutually illustrate each other. When He healed bodily blindness, it was a type of the healing of the inner eye; when He raised the dead, He meant to suggest that He was the Resurrection and the Life in the spiritual world as well; when He cleansed the leper, His triumph spoke of another over the leprosy of sin; when He multiplied the loaves, He followed the miracle with a discourse on the Bread of Life; when He stilled the storm, it was an assurance that He could speak peace to the troubled conscience.

82. Thus His miracles were a natural and essential part of His messianic work. They were an excellent means of making Him known to the nation. They bound those whom He cured to Him with strong ties of gratitude; and without doubt, in many cases, the faith in Him as a miracle-worker led to a higher faith. So it was in the case of His devoted follower Mary Magdalene, out of whom He cast seven devils.

83. To Jesus this work must have brought both great pain and great joy. To His tender and exquisitely sympathetic heart, that never grew callous in the least degree, it must often have been harrowing to mingle with so much disease, and to see the awful effects of sin. But He was in the right place; it suited His great love to be where help was needed. And what a joy it must have been to Him to distribute blessings on every hand and erase the traces of sin; to see health returning beneath His touch; to meet the joyous and grateful glances of the opening eyes; to hear the blessings of mothers and sisters, as He restored their loved ones to their arms; and to see the light of love and welcome in the faces of the poor, as He entered their towns and villages. He drank deeply of the well at which He would have His followers to be ever drinking—the bliss of doing good.

THE TEACHER

84. The other great instrument with which Jesus did His work was His teaching. It was by far the more important of the two. His miracles were only the bell tolled to bring the people to hear His words. They impressed those who might not yet be susceptible to the subtler influence, and brought them within its range.

85. The miracles probably made most noise, but His preaching also spread His fame far and wide. There is no power whose attraction is more unfailing than that of the eloquent word. Barbarians, listening to their bards and storytellers, Greeks, listening to the restrained passion of their orators, and matter-of-fact nations like the Roman, have alike acknowledged its power to be irresistible. The Jews prized it above almost every other attraction, and among the figures of their mighty dead none were revered more highly than the prophets—those eloquent utterers of the truth whom heaven had sent them from age to age. Though the Baptist performed no miracles, multitudes flocked to him, because in his accents they recognized the thunder of this power, which for so many generations no Jewish ear had listened to. Jesus also was recognized as a prophet, and accordingly His preaching created widespread excitement. "He spake in their synagogues, being glorified of all." His words were heard with wonder and amazement. Sometimes the multitude on the beach of the lake so pressed upon Him to hear, that He had to enter into a ship and address them from the deck, as they spread themselves out in a semicircle on the ascending shore. His enemies themselves bore witness that "never man spake like this"; and, meager as are the remains of His preaching that we possess, they are amply sufficient to make us echo the sentiment and understand the impression that He produced. All His words together that have been preserved to us would not occupy more space in print than half-a-dozen ordinary sermons; yet it is not too much to say that they are the most precious literary heritage of the human race. His words, like His miracles, were expressions of Himself, and every one of them has in it something of the grandeur of His character.

86. The form of the preaching of Jesus was essentially Jewish. The Oriental mind does not work in the same way as the mind of the West. Our thinking and speaking, when at their best, are fluent, expansive, closely reasoned. The kind of discourse that we admire is one that takes up an important subject, divides it into different branches, treats it fully under each of the heads, closely articulates part to part, and closes with a moving appeal to the feelings, so as to sway the will to some practical result. The Oriental mind, on the contrary, loves to brood long on a single point, to turn it over and over, to gather up all the truth about it into a focus, and pour it in a few pointed and memorable words. It is concise, epigrammatic, oracular. A Western speaker's discourse is a systematic structure, or like a chain in which link is firmly knit to link; an Oriental's is like the sky at night, full of innumerable burning points shining forth from a dark background.

87. Such was the form of the teaching of Jesus. It consisted of numerous sayings, every one of which contained the greatest possible amount of truth in the smallest possible compass, and was expressed in language so concise and pointed as to stick in the memory like an arrow. Read them, and you will find that every one of them, as you ponder it, sucks the mind in like a whirlpool, until it is lost in the depths. You will find, too, that there are very few of them that you do not know by heart. They have found their way into the memory of Christendom as no other words have done. Even before the meaning has been apprehended, the perfect, proverb-like expression lodges itself fast in the mind.

88. But there was another characteristic of the form of Jesus' teaching. It was full of figures of speech. He thought in images. He had ever been a loving and accurate observer of nature around Him—of the colors of the flowers, the ways of the birds, the growth of the trees, the

vicissitudes of the seasons—and was an equally keen observer of the ways of men in all parts of life—in religion, in business, in the home. The result was that He could neither think nor speak without His thought running into the mold of some natural image. His preaching was alive with such references, and therefore full of color, movement, and changing forms. There were no abstract statements in it; they were all changed into pictures. Thus, in His sayings, we can still see the aspects of the country and the life of the time as in a panorama—the lilies, whose gorgeous beauty His eyes feasted on, waving in the fields; the sheep following the shepherd; the broad and narrow city gates; the virgins with their lamps awaiting in the darkness the bridal procession; the Pharisee with his broad phylacteries and the publican with bent head at prayer together in the temple; the rich man seated in his palace at a feast, and the beggar lying at his gate with the dogs licking his sores; and a hundred other pictures that lay bare the inner and minute life of the time, over which history in general sweeps heedlessly with majestic stride.

89. But the most characteristic form of speech He made use of was the parable. It was a combination of the two qualities already mentioned—concise, memorable expression, and a figurative style. It used an incident, taken from common life and rounded into a gem-like picture, to set forth some corresponding truth in the higher and spiritual region. It was a favorite Jewish mode of stating truth, but Jesus imparted to it by far the richest and most perfect development. About one-third of all His sayings that have been preserved to us consists of parables. This shows how they stuck in the memory. In the same way the hearers of the sermons of any preacher will probably, after a few years, remember the illustrations they have contained far better than anything else in them. How these parables have remained in the memory of all

generations since! The Prodigal Son, the Sower, the Ten Virgins, the Good Samaritan—these and many others are pictures hung up in millions of minds. What passages in the greatest masters of expression—in Homer, in Virgil, in Dante, in Shakespeare—have secured for themselves so universal a hold on men, or been felt to be so fadelessly fresh and true? He never went far for His illustrations. As a master of painting will make for you, with a morsel of chalk or a burnt stick, a face at which you must laugh or weep or wonder, so Jesus took the commonest objects and incidents around Him—the sewing of a piece of cloth on an old garment, the bursting of an old bottle, the children playing in the marketplace at weddings and funerals, or the tumbling of a hut in a storm—to change them into perfect pictures and make them the vehicles for conveying to the world immortal truth. No wonder the crowds followed Him! Even the simplest could delight in such pictures and carry away as a life-long possession the expression at least of His ideas, though it might require the thought of centuries to pierce their crystalline depths. Never was speaking so simple yet so profound, so pictorial yet so absolutely true.

90. Such were the qualities of His style. The qualities of the Preacher Himself have been preserved to us in the criticism of His hearers, and are manifest in the remains of His addresses that the Gospels contain.

91. The most prominent of them seems to have been *authority:* "The people were astonished at his doctrine, for he taught them as one having authority, and not as the scribes." The first thing that struck His hearers was the contrast between His words and the preaching they were likely to hear from the scribes in the synagogues. These were the exponents of the deadest and driest system of theology that has ever passed in any age for religion. Instead of expounding the Scriptures, which were in their hands, and would have lent living power to their words, they retailed the opinions of commentators, and were afraid to advance any statement unless it was backed by the authority of some master. Instead of dwelling on the great themes of justice and mercy, love and God, they tortured the sacred text into a ceremonial manual, and preached on the proper breadth of phylacteries, the proper postures for prayer, the proper length of fasts, the distance that might be walked on the Sabbath, and so forth; for in these things the religion of the time consisted. In order to see anything in modern times at all like the preaching that then prevailed, we must go back to the Reformation period, when, as the historian of Knox tells us, the harangues delivered by the monks were empty, ridiculous, and wretched in the extreme. "Legendary tales concerning the founder of some religious order, the miracles he performed, his combats with the devil, his watchings, fastings, flagellations; the virtues of holy water, chrism, crossing, and exorcism; the horrors of purgatory, and the numbers released from it by the intercessions of some powerful saint—these, with low jests, table-talk, and fireside scandal, formed the favorite topics of the preachers, and were served up to the people instead of the pure, salutary, and sublime doctrines of the Bible." Perhaps the contrast that the Scottish people three and a half centuries ago felt between such harangues and the noble words of Wishart and Knox, may convey to our mind as good an idea as can be gotten of the effect of the preaching of Jesus on His contemporaries. He knew nothing of the authority of masters and schools of interpretation, but spoke as one whose own eyes had gazed on the objects of the eternal world. He needed none to tell Him of God or of man, for He knew both perfectly. He was possessed with the sense of a mission, which drove Him on and imparted earnestness to every word and

gesture. He knew Himself sent from God, and the words
He spoke to be not His own, but God's. He did not hesitate to tell those who neglected His words that in the
judgment they would be condemned by the Ninevites
and the Queen of Sheba, who had listened to Jonah and
Solomon, for they were hearing One greater than any
prophet or king. He warned them that on their acceptance
or rejection of the message He bore would depend their
future joy or sadness. This was the tone of earnestness, of
majesty and authority that struck His hearers with awe.

92. Another quality that the people remarked in Him
was *boldness:* "Lo, he speaketh boldly." This appeared
more wonderful because He was an unlettered man, one
who had not passed through the schools of Jerusalem, or
received the stamp of any earthly authority. But this
quality came from the same source as His authoritative-
ness. Timidity usually springs from self-consciousness.
The preacher who is afraid of his audience, and respects
the persons of the learned and the great, is thinking of
himself and of what will be said of his performance. But
he who feels himself driven on by a divine mission
forgets himself. All audiences are alike to him, be they
gentle or simple; he is thinking only of the message he has
to deliver. Jesus was ever looking the spiritual and eternal
realities in the face; the spell of their greatness held Him,
and all human distinctions disappeared in their presence;
men of every class were only men to Him. He was borne
along on the torrent of His mission, and what might happen to Him could not make Him stop to question or tremble. He discovered His boldness chiefly in attacking the
abuses and ideals of the time. It would be a complete
mistake to think of Him as all mildness and meekness.
There is scarcely any element more conspicuous in His
words than a strain of fierce indignation. It was an age of
shams above almost any that have ever been. They oc-

cupied all high places. They paraded themselves in social life, occupied the chairs of learning, and above all debased every part of religion. Hypocrisy had become so universal that it had ceased even to doubt itself. The ideals of the people were utterly mean and mistaken. One can feel throbbing through His words, from first to last, an indignation against all this, which had begun with His earliest observation in Nazareth and ripened with His increasing knowledge of the times. The things that were highly esteemed among men, He broadly asserted, were abomination in the sight of God. There never was in the history of speech a polemic so scathing, so annihilating, as His against the figures to which the reverence of the multitude had been paid before His withering words fell on them—the scribe, the Pharisee, the priest, and the Levite.

93. A third quality that His hearers remarked about was *power:* "His word was with power." This was the result of that unction of the Holy One, without which even the most solemn truths fall on the ear without effect. He was filled with the Spirit without measure. Therefore the truth possessed Him. It burned and swelled in His own bosom, and He proclaimed from heart to heart. He had the Spirit not only in such degree as to fill Himself, but also so as to be able to impart it to others. It overflowed with His words and seized the souls of His hearers, filling with enthusiasm the mind and the heart.

94. A fourth quality that was observed in His preaching, and was surely a very prominent one, was *graciousness:* "They wondered at the gracious words which proceeded out of his mouth." In spite of His tone of authority and His fearless and scathing attacks on the times, there was diffused over all He said a glow of grace and love. Here especially His character spoke. How could

He who was the incarnation of love help letting the glow and warmth of the heavenly fire that dwelt in Him spread over His words? The scribes of the time were hard, proud, and loveless. They flattered the rich and honored the learned, but of the great mass of their hearers they said, "This people, which knoweth not the law, is cursed." But to Jesus every soul was infinitely precious. It did not matter under what humble dress or social deformity the pearl was hidden; it did not even matter beneath what rubbish and filth of sin it was buried; He never missed it for a moment. Therefore He spoke to His hearers of every grade with the same respect. Surely it was the divine love itself, uttering itself from the innermost recess of the divine being, that spoke in the parables of the fifteenth chapter of Luke.

95. Such were some of the qualities of the Preacher. And one more may be mentioned, which may be said to embrace all the rest, and is perhaps the highest quality of public speech. He *addressed men as men*, not as members of any class or possessors of any peculiar culture. The differences that divide men, such as wealth, rank, and education, are on the surface. The elements in which they are all alike—the broad sense of the understanding, the great passions of the heart, the primary instincts of the conscience—are profound. Not that these are the same in all men. In some they are deeper, in others shallower; but in all they are far deeper than anything else. He who addresses them appeals to the depths in His hearers. He will be equally intelligible to all. Every hearer will receive his own portion from Him; the small and shallow mind will get as much as it can take, and the largest and deepest will get its fill at the same feast. This is why the words of Jesus are perennial in their freshness. They are for all generations, and equally for all. They appeal to the deepest elements in human nature today in England or

China as much as they did in Palestine when they were
spoken.

96. When we come to inquire what the matter of
Jesus' preaching consisted of, we perhaps naturally expect
to find Him expounding the system of doctrine that we
are ourselves acquainted with, in the forms, say, of the
Catechism or the Confession of Faith. But what we find is
very different. He did not make use of any system of
doctrine. We can scarcely doubt that all the numerous and
varied ideas of His preaching, as well as those which He
never expressed, coexisted in His mind as one world of
rounded truth. But they did not so coexist in His teaching.
He did not use theological phraseology, speaking of the
Trinity, of predestination, of effectual calling, although
the ideas that these terms cover underlay His words, and
it is the undoubted task of science to bring them forth. But
He spoke in the language of life, and concentrated His
preaching on a few burning points that touched the heart,
the conscience, and the time.

97. The central idea and the most common phrase of
His preaching was "the kingdom of God." It will be remembered how many of His parables begin with "The
kingdom of heaven is like" so and so. He said, "I must
preach the kingdom of God to other cities also," thereby
characterizing the matter of His preaching; and in the
same way He is said to have sent forth the apostles "to
preach the kingdom of God." He did not invent the
phrase. It was a historical one handed down from the
past, and was common in the mouths of His contemporaries. The Baptist had made large use of it, the burden
of his message being, "The kingdom of God is at hand."

98. What did it signify? It meant the new era, which
the prophets had predicted and the saints had looked for.

Jesus announced that it had come, and that He had brought it. The time of waiting was fulfilled. Many prophets and righteous men, He told His contemporaries, had desired to see the things they saw, but had not seen them. He declared that so great were the privileges and glories of the new era, that the least partaker of them was greater than the Baptist, though he had been the greatest representative of the old era.

99. All this was no more than His contemporaries would have expected to hear, if they had recognized that the kingdom of God was really come. But they looked around, and asked where the new era was that Jesus said He had brought. Here He and they were at complete variance. They emphasized the first part of the phrase, "the kingdom," He the second, "of God." They expected the new era to appear in magnificent material forms—in a kingdom of which God indeed was to be the Ruler, but which was to show itself in worldly splendor, in force of arms, in a universal empire. Jesus saw the new era in an empire of God over the loving heart and the obedient will. They looked for it outside; He said, "It is within you." They looked for a period of external glory and happiness; He placed the glory and blessedness of the new time in character. So He began His Sermon on the Mount, that great manifesto of the new era, with a series of "Blesseds." But the blessedness was entirely that of character. And it was a character totally different from that which was then looked up to as imparting glory and happiness to its possessor—that of the proud Pharisee, the wealthy Sadducee, or the learned scribe. Blessed, said He, are the poor in spirit, they who mourn, the meek, they who hunger and thirst after righteousness, the merciful, the pure in heart, the peacemakers, they who are persecuted for righteousness' sake.

100. The main drift of His preaching was to set forth this conception of the kingdom of God, the character of its members, their blessedness in the love and communion of their Father in heaven, and their prospects in the glory of the future world. He exhibited the contrast between it and the formal religion of the time, with its lack of spirituality and its substitution of ceremonial observances for character. He invited all classes into the kingdom—the rich by showing, as in the parable of the Rich Man and Lazarus, the vanity and danger of seeking their blessedness in wealth; and the poor by penetrating them with the sense of their dignity, persuading them with the most overflowing affection and winning words that the only true wealth was in character, and assuring them that, if they sought first the kingdom of God, their heavenly Father, who fed the ravens and clothed the lilies, would not allow them to be in need.

101. But the center and soul of His preaching was Himself. He contained within Himself the new era. He not only announced it, but created it. The new character that made men subjects of the kingdom and sharers of its privileges was to be gotten from Him alone. Therefore the practical issue of every address of Christ was the command to come to Him, to learn of Him, to follow Him. "Come unto me, all ye that labour and are heavy laden," was the keynote, the deepest and final word of all His discourses.

102. It is impossible to read the discourses of Jesus without remarking that, wonderful as they are, yet some of the most characteristic doctrines of Christianity, as it is set forth in the epistles of Paul and now cherished in the minds of the most devoted and enlightened Christians, hold a very inconsiderable place in them. Especially is this the case in regard to the great doctrines of the gospel as to how a sinner is reconciled to God, and how, in a pardoned soul, the character is gradually produced which makes it like Christ and pleasing to the Father. The lack of reference to such doctrines may indeed be much exaggerated, the fact being that there is not one prominent doctrine of the great apostle the germs of which are not to be found in the teaching of Christ Himself. Yet the contrast is marked enough to have given some color for denying that the distinctive doctrines of Paul are genuine elements of Christianity. But the true explanation of the phenomenon is very different. Jesus was not a mere teacher. His character was greater than His words, and so was His work. The chief part of that work was to atone for the sins of the world by His death on the cross. But His nearest followers never would believe that He was to die, and, until His death happened, it was impossible to explain its far-reaching significance. Paul's most distinctive doctrines are merely expositions of the meaning of two great facts—the death of Christ and the mission of the Spirit by the glorified Redeemer. It is obvious that these facts could not be fully explained in the words of Jesus Himself, when they had not yet taken place; but to suppress the inspired explanation of them would be to extinguish the light of the gospel and rob Christ of His crowning glory.

103. Jesus' audience varied greatly both in size and character on different occasions. Frequently it was the great multitude. He addressed them everywhere—on the mountain, on the seashore, on the highway, in the synagogues, in the temple courts. But He was as willing to speak with a single individual, however humble. He seized every opportunity to do so. Although He was worn out with fatigue, He talked to the woman at the well; He received Nicodemus alone; He taught Mary in her home. There are said to be nineteen such private interviews mentioned in the Gospels. They leave to His followers a

memorable example. This is perhaps the most effective of
all forms of instruction, as it is certainly the best test of
earnestness. A man who preaches to thousands with enthusiasm may be a mere orator, but the man who seeks
opportunities of speaking closely on the welfare of their
souls to individuals must have a real fire from heaven
burning in his heart.

104. Often His audience consisted of the circle of His
disciples. His preaching divided His hearers. He has
Himself, in such parables as the Sower, the Tares and
the Wheat, and the Wedding Feast, described with une-
qualed vividness its effects on different classes. Some it
utterly repelled; others heard it with wonder, without being
touched in the heart; others were affected for a time, but
soon returned to their old interests. It is terrible to think
how few there were, even when the Son of God was
preaching, who heard unto salvation. Those who did so,
gradually formed around Him a body of disciples. They
followed Him about, hearing all His discourses, and often
He spoke to them alone. Such were the five hundred to
whom He appeared in Galilee after His resurrection.
Some of them were women, such as Mary Magdalene,
Susanna, and Joanna the wife of Herod's steward, who,
being wealthy, gladly supplied His few simple needs. To
these disciples He gave a more thorough instruction than
to the crowd. He explained to them in private whatever
was obscure in His public teaching. More than once He
made the strange statement that He spoke in parables to
the multitudes in order that, though hearing, they might
not understand. This could only mean that those who had
no real interest in the truth were sent away with the mere
beautiful shell, but that the obscurity was intended to
provoke to further inquiry, as a veil half-drawn over a
beautiful face intensifies the desire to see it; and to those
who had a spiritual craving for more He gladly communi-

cated the hidden secret. These, when the nation as a whole declared itself unworthy of being the medium of the Messiah's world-wide influence, became the nucleus of that spiritual society, elevated above all local limitations and distinctions of rank and nationality, in which the spirit and doctrine of Christ were to be spread and perpetuated in the world.

THE APOSTOLATE

105. Perhaps the formation of the Apostolate ought to be placed side by side with miracles and preaching as a third means by which He did His work. The men who became the twelve apostles were at first only ordinary disciples like many others. This, at least, was the position of such of them as were already His followers during the first year of His ministry. At the opening of His Galilean activity, their attachment to Him entered on a second stage; He called them to give up their ordinary employments and be with Him constantly. And probably not many weeks later He promoted them to the third and final stage of nearness to Himself, by ordaining them to be apostles.

106. It was when His work grew so extensive and pressing that it was quite impossible for Him to overtake it all, that He multiplied Himself, so to speak, by appointing them His assistants. He commissioned them to teach the simpler elements of His doctrine and conferred on them miraculous powers similar to His own. In this way many towns were evangelized which He had not had time to visit, and many persons cured who could not have been brought into contact with Him. But, as future events proved, His aims in their appointment were much more far-reaching. His work was for all time and for the whole world. It could not be accomplished in a single lifetime. He foresaw this, and made provision for it by the early choice of agents who might take up His plans after He was gone, and in whom He might still extend His influence over mankind. He Himself wrote nothing. It may be thought that writing would have been the best way of perpetuating His influence and giving the world a perfect image of Himself; and we cannot help imagining with a glow of strong desire what a volume penned by His hand would have been. But for wise reasons He abstained from this kind of work and resolved to live after death in the lives of chosen men.

107. It is surprising to see what sort of persons He selected for so grand a destiny. They did not belong to the influential and learned classes. No doubt the heads and leaders of the nation ought to have been the organs of their Messiah, but they proved themselves totally unworthy of the great vocation. He was able to do without them; He did not need the influence of carnal power and wisdom. Ever desirous to work with the elements of character that are not bound to any station of life or grade of culture, He did not hesitate to commit His cause to twelve simple men, destitute of learning and belonging to the common people. He made the selection after a night spent in prayer, and doubtless after many days of deliberation. The event showed with what insight into character He had acted. They turned out to be instruments thoroughly fitted for the great design; two at least, John and Peter, were men of supreme gifts; and, though one turned out a traitor, and the choice of him will probably, after all explanations, ever remain a partially explained mystery, yet the selection of agents who were at first so unlikely, but in the end proved so successful, will always be one of the chief monuments of the incomparable originality of Jesus.

108. It would, however, be a very inadequate account of His relation to the Twelve merely to point out the insight with which He discerned in them the germs of fitness for their grand future. They became very great men, and in the founding of the Christian Church achieved a work of immeasurable importance. They may be said, in a sense they little dreamed of, to sit on thrones ruling the modern world. They stand like a row of noble pillars towering afar across the flats of time. But the sunlight that shines on them, and makes them visible, comes entirely from Him. He gave them all their greatness; and theirs is one of the most striking evidences of His. What must He have been whose influence imparted to them such magnitude of character and made them fit for so gigantic a task! At first they were rude and carnal in the extreme. What hope was there that they would ever be able to appreciate the designs of a mind like His, to inherit His work, to possess in any degree a spirit so exquisite, and transmit to future generations a faithful image of His character? But He educated them with the most affectionate patience, bearing with their vulgar hopes and their clumsy misunderstandings of His meaning. Never forgetting for a moment the part they were to play in the future, He made their training His most constant work. They were much more constantly in His company than even the general body of His disciples, seeing all He did in public and hearing all He said. They were often His ownly audience, and then He unveiled to them the glories and mysteries of His doctrine, sowing in their minds the seeds of truth, which time and experience were by and by to bear fruit. But the most important part of their training was one that was perhaps at the time little noticed, though it was producing splendid results—the silent and constant influence of His character on theirs. He drew them to Himself and stamped His own image on them. It was this that made them the men they became.

For this, more than all else, the generations of those who love Him look back to them with envy. We admire and adore at a distance the qualities of His character; but what must it have been to see them in the unity of life, and for years to feel their molding pressure! Can we recall with any fullness the features of this character whose glory they beheld and under whose power they lived?

THE HUMAN CHARACTER OF JESUS

109. Perhaps the most obvious feature they would remark in Him was *purposefulness*. This certainly is the ground tone that sounds in all His sayings that have been preserved to us, and the pulse that we feel beating in all His recorded actions. He was possessed with a purpose that guided and drove Him on. Most lives aim at nothing in particular but drift along, under the influence of varying moods and instincts or on the currents of society, and achieve nothing. But Jesus evidently had a definite object before Him, which absorbed His thoughts and drew out His energies. He would often give as a reason for not doing something, "Mine hour is not yet come," as if His design absorbed every moment, and every hour had its own allotted part of the task. This imparted an earnestness and rapidity of execution to His life that most lives altogether lack. It saved Him, too, from the dispersion of energy on details, and carefulness about little things, on which those who obey no definite call throw themselves away, and made His life, various as were its activities, an unbroken unity.

110. Closely connected with this quality was another prominent one, which may be called *faith,* and by which is meant His astonishing confidence in the accomplishment of His purpose, and apparent disregard both of means and opposition. If it be considered in the most general way how vast His aim was—to reform His nation and begin an everlasting and world-wide religious movement; if the opposition that He encountered, and foresaw His cause would have to meet at every stage of its progress, be considered; and if it be remembered what, as a man, He was—an unlettered Galilean peasant—His quiet and unwavering confidence in His success will appear only less remarkable than His success itself. After reading the Gospels through, one asks in wonder what He did to produce so mighty an impression on the world. He constructed no elaborate machinery to ensure the effect. He did not lay hold of the centers of influence—learning, wealth, government, etc. It is true He instituted the church. But He left no detailed explanations of its nature or rules for its constitution. This was the simplicity of faith, which does not contrive and prepare, but simply goes forward and does the work. It was the quality that He said could remove mountains, and that he chiefly desired in His followers. This was the foolishness of the gospel, of which Paul boasted, as it was going forth, in the recklessness of power, but with laughable meagerness of equipment, to overcome the Greek and Roman world.

111. A third prominent feature of His character was *originality*. Most lives are easily explained. They are mere products of circumstances, and copies of thousands like them that surround or have preceded them. The habits and customs of the country to which we belong, the fashions and tastes of our generation, the traditions of our education, the prejudices of our class, the opinions of our school or sect—these form us. We do work determined for us by a fortuitous concourse of circumstances; our convictions are fixed on us by authority from without, instead of growing naturally from within; our opinions are blown to us in fragments on every wind. But what circumstances made the Man Christ Jesus? There never was an age more dry and barren than that in which He was born. He was like a tall, fresh palm springing out of a desert. What was there in the petty life of Nazareth to produce so gigantic a character? How could the notoriously wicked village send forth such breathing purity? It may have been that a scribe taught Him the vocables and grammar of knowledge, but His doctrine was a complete contradiction of all that the scribes taught. The fashions of the sects never laid hold of His free spirit. How clearly, amidst the sounds that filled the ears of His time, He heard the neglected voice of truth, which was quite different from them! How clearly, behind all the pretentious and accepted forms of piety, He saw the lovely and neglected figure of real godliness! He cannot be explained by anything that was in the world and might have produced Him. He grew from within. He directed His eyes straight on the facts of nature and life and believed what He saw, instead of allowing His vision to be tutored by what others had said they saw. He was equally loyal to the truth in His words. He went forth and spoke out without hesitation what He believed, though it shook to their foundations the institutions, the creeds and customs of His country, and loosened the opinions of the populace in a hundred points in which they had been educated. It may indeed be said that, though the Jewish nation of His own time was an utterly dry ground, out of which no green and great thing could be expected to grow, He reverted to the earlier history of His nation and nourished His mind on the ideas of Moses and the prophets. There is some truth in this. But, affectionate and constant as was His familiarity with them, He handled them with a free and fearless hand. He redeemed them from themselves and exhibited in perfection the ideas that they taught only in germ. What a contrast between the covenant God of Israel and the Father in heaven whom He revealed; between the temple, with its priests and bloody sacrifices, and the worship in spirit and in truth; between the national and ceremonial morality of the Law and the morality of the conscience and the heart! Even in comparison with the figures of Moses, Elijah, and Isaiah, He towers aloft in lonely originality.

112. A fourth and very glorious feature of His character was *love to men*. It has been already said that He was possessed with an overmastering purpose. But beneath a great life purpose there must be a great passion, which shapes and sustains it. Love to men was the passion that directed and inspired Him. How it sprang up and grew in the seclusion of Nazareth, and on what materials it fed, we have not been informed with any detail. We only know that, when He appeared in public, it was a master passion, which completely swallowed up self-love, filled Him with boundless pity for human misery, and enabled Him to go forward without once looking back in the undertaking to which He had devoted Himself. We know only in general that it drew its support from the conception that He had of the infinite value of the human soul. It went beyond all the limits that other men have put to their benevolence. Differences of class and nationality usually cool men's interest in each other; in nearly all countries it has been considered a virtue to hate enemies; and it is generally agreed to loathe and avoid those who have outraged the laws of respectability. But He paid no heed to these conventions; the overpowering sense of the preciousness that He perceived in enemy, foreigner, and outcast alike, forbade Him. This marvelous love shaped the purpose of His life. It gave Him the most tender and intense sympathy with every form of pain and misery. It was His deepest reason for adopting the calling of a healer. Wherever help was most needed, there His merciful heart drew Him. But it was especially to save the soul that His love impelled Him. He knew this was the real jewel, which everything should be done to rescue, and that its miseries and perils were the most dangerous of all. There has sometimes been love to others without this vital aim. But His love was directed by wisdom to the truest need of those He loved. He knew He was doing His very best for them when He was saving them from their sins.

113. But the crowning attribute of His human character was *love to God*. It is the supreme honor and attainment of man to be one with God in feeling, thought, and purpose. Jesus had this in perfection. To us it is difficult to realize God. The mass of men scarcely think about Him at all; and even the godliest confess that it costs them severe effort to discipline their minds into the habit of constantly realizing Him. When we do think of Him, it is with a painful sense of a disharmony between what is in us and what is in Him. We cannot remain, even for a few minutes, in His presence without the sense, in greater or less degree, that His thoughts are not our thoughts, nor His ways our ways. With Jesus it was not so. He realized God always. He never spent an hour, He never did an action, without direct reference to Him. God was about Him like the atmosphere He breathed or the sunlight in which He walked. His thoughts were God's thoughts; His desires were never in the least different from God's; His purpose, He was perfectly sure, was God's purpose for Him. How did He attain this absolute harmony with God? To a large extent it must be attributed to the perfect harmony of His nature within itself, yet in some measure He got it by the same means by which we laboriously seek it—by the study of God's thoughts and purposes in His Word, which, from His childhood, was His constant delight; by cultivating all His life long the habit of prayer for which He found time even when He did not have time to eat; and by patiently resisting temptations to entertain thoughts and purposes of His own different from God's. This it was which gave Him such faith and fearlessness in His work; He knew that the call to do it had come from God, and that He was immortal until it was done. This was what made Him, with all His self-consciousness and originality, the pattern of meekness and submission; for He was forever bringing every thought and wish into obedience to His Father's will. This was the secret of the peace and majestic calmness that imparted such a grandeur to His demeanor in the most trying hours of life. He knew that the worst that could happen to Him was His Father's will for Him; and this was enough. He always had at hand a retreat of perfect rest, silence, and sunshine, into which he could retire from the clamor and confusion around Him. This was the great secret he bequeathed to His followers, when He said to them at parting, "Peace I leave with you; my peace I give unto you."

114. The sinlessness of Jesus has been often dwelt on as the crowning attribute of His character. The Scriptures, which so frankly record the errors of their greatest heroes, such as Abraham and Moses, have no sins of His to record. There is no more prominent characteristic of the saints of antiquity than their penitence: the more supremely saintly they were, the more abundant and bitter were their tears and lamentations over their sinfulness. But, although it is acknowledged by all that Jesus was the supreme religious figure of history, He never exhibited this characteristic of saintliness; He confessed no sin. Must it not have been because He had no sin to confess? Yet the idea of sinlessness is too negative to express the perfection of His character. He was sinless; but He was so because He was absolutely full of love. Sin against God is merely the expression of lack of love to God, and sin against man of lack of love to man. A being quite full of love to both God and man cannot possibly sin against either. This fullness of love to His Father and His fellow-men, ruling every expression of His being, constituted the perfection of His character.

115. To the impression produced on them by their long-continued contact with their Master the Twelve owed all they became. We cannot trace with any certainty at what time they began to realize the central truth of the Christianity they were afterward to publish to the world, that behind the tenderness and majesty of this human character there was in Him something still more august, or by what stages their impressions ripened to the full conviction that in Him perfect manhood was in union with perfect Deity. This was the goal of all the revelations of Himself that He made to them. But the breakdown of their faith at His death shows how immature up until that time must have been their convictions in regard to His personality, however worthily they were able, in certain happy hours, to express their faith in Him. It was the experience of the Resurrection and Ascension that gave to the fluid impressions, which had long been accumulating in their minds, the touch by which they were made to crystallize into the immovable conviction, that in Him with whom it had been given to them to associate so intimately, God was manifest in the flesh.

6

THE YEAR
OF OPPOSITION

116. For a whole year Jesus pursued His work in Galilee with incessant energy, moving among the pitiable crowds that solicited His miraculous help, and seizing every opportunity of pouring His words of grace and truth into the ears of the multitude or of the solitary anxious inquirer. In hundreds of homes, to whose inmates he had restored health and joy, His name must have become a household word; in thousands of minds, whose depths His preaching had stirred, He must have been cherished with gratitude and love. Wider and wider rang the echoes of His fame. For a time it seemed as if all Galilee was to become His disciples, and as if the movement so started might easily roll southward, overbearing all opposition and enveloping the whole land in an enthusiasm of love for the Healer and of obedience to the Teacher.

117. But the twelve months had scarcely passed when it became sadly evident that this was not to be. The Galilean mind turned out to be stony ground, where the seed of the kingdom rushed up quickly, but just as quickly withered away. The change was sudden and complete, and at once altered all the features of the life of Jesus. He lingered in Galilee for six months longer; but these months were very unlike the first twelve. The voices that rose around Him were no longer the ringing shouts of gratitude and applause, but voices of opposition, bitter and blasphemous. He was no longer to be seen moving from one populous place to another in the heart of the country, welcomed everywhere by those who waited to experience or to see His miracles, and followed by thousands eager not to lose a word of His discourses. He was a fugitive, seeking the most distant and outlandish places and accompanied only by a handful of followers. At the end of the six months He left Galilee forever, but not, as might at one time have been anticipated, borne aloft on the wave of public acknowledgment, to make an easy conquest of the hearts of the southern part of the country and take victorious possession of a Jerusalem unable to resist the unanimous voice of the people. He did, indeed, labor for six months more in the southern part of the land—in Judaea and Peraea; nor were there seen, where His miracles were performed for the first time, the same signs of public enthusiasm as had greeted Him in the first months of joy in Galilee; but the most that He effected was to add a few to the company of His faithful disciples. He did, from the day He left Galilee, set His face stedfastly toward Jerusalem; and the six months He spent in Peraea and Judaea may be regarded as occupied with a slow journey there; but the journey was begun in the full assurance, which He openly expressed to the disciples, that in the capital He was to receive no triumph over enthusiastic hearts and minds convinced, but to meet with a final national rejection and be killed instead of crowned.

118. We must trace the causes and the progress of this change in the sentiment of the Galileans, and this sad turn in the career of Jesus.

119. From the first the learned and influential classes had taken up an attitude of opposition to Him. The more worldly sections of them, indeed—the Sadducees and Herodians—for a long time paid little attention to Him. They had their own affairs to mind—their wealth, their court influence, their amusements. They cared little for a religious movement going on among the lower orders. The public rumor that one professing to be the Messiah had appeared did not excite their interest, for they did not share the popular expectations on the subject. They said to each other that this was only one more of the pretenders whom the peculiar ideas of the populace were sure to raise up from time to time. It was only when the movement seemed to them to be threatening to lead to a political revolt, which would bring down the iron hand of their Roman masters on the country, afford the procurator an excuse for new extortions, and imperil their property and comforts, that they roused themselves to pay any attention to Him.

120. It was different, however, with the more religious sections of the upper class—the Pharisees and scribes. They took the deepest interest in all ecclesiastical and religious phenomena. A movement of a religious kind among the populace excited their eager attention, for they themselves aimed for popular influence. A new voice with the ring of prophecy in it, or the promulgation of any new doctrine or tenet, caught their ear at once. But, above all, any one putting himself forward as the Messiah produced the utmost ferment among them; for they ardently cherished messianic hopes and were at the time smarting sharply under the foreign domination. In relation to the rest of the community, they corresponded to our clergy and leading religious laymen, and probably formed about the same proportion of the population, and exercised at least as great an influence as these do among us. It has been estimated that they may have numbered about six thousand. They passed for the best persons in the country, the conservators of respectability and orthodoxy; and the masses looked up to them as those who had the right to judge and determine in all religious matters.

121. They cannot be accused of having neglected Jesus. They turned their earnest attention to Him from the first. They followed Him step by step. They discussed His doctrines and His claims, and made up their minds. Their decision was adverse, and they followed it up with acts, never becoming remiss in their activity for an hour.

122. This is perhaps the most solemn and appalling circumstance in the whole tragedy of the life of Christ, that the men who rejected, hunted down and murdered Him, were those reputed the best in the nation, its teachers and examples, the zealous conservators of the Bible and the traditions of the past—men who were eagerly waiting for the Messiah, who judged Jesus, as they believed, according to the Scriptures, and thought they were obeying the dictates of conscience and doing God service when they treated Him as they did. There cannot fail sometimes to sweep across the mind of a reader of the Gospels a strong feeling of pity for them, and a kind of sympathy with them. Jesus was so unlike the Messiah whom they were looking for and their fathers had taught them to expect! He so completely traversed their prejudices and maxims, and dishonored so many things that they had been taught to regard as sacred! They may surely be pitied; there never was a crime like their crime, and there was never punishment like their punishment. There is the same sadness about the fate of those who are thrown upon any great crisis of the world's history and, not understanding the signs of the times, make fatal mistakes; as those did, for example, who at the Reformation were unable to go forth and join the march of Providence.

123. Yet, at the bottom, what was their case? It was just this, that they were so blinded with sin that they could not discern the light. Their views of the Messiah had been distorted by centuries of worldliness and unspirituality, of which they were the like-minded heirs. They thought Jesus a sinner, because He did not conform to ordinances that they and their fathers had profanely

added to those of God's Word, and because their conception of a good man, to which He did not answer, was
utterly false. Jesus supplied them with evidence enough,
but He could not give them eyes to see it. There is a
something at the bottom of hearts that are honest and true
which, however long and deeply it may have been buried
under prejudice and sin, leaps up with joy and desires to
embrace what is true, what is reverent, what is pure and
great, when it draws near. But nothing of the kind was
found in them; their hearts were seared, hardened, and
dead. They brought their stock rules and arbitrary
standards to judge Him by, and were never shaken by His
greatness from the fatal attitude of criticism. He brought
truth near them, but they did not have the truth-loving
ear to recognize the enchanting sound. He brought the
whitest purity, such as archangels would have veiled their
faces at, near them, but they were not overawed. He
brought near them the very face of mercy and heavenly
love, but their dim eyes made no response. We may indeed pity the conduct of such men as an appalling misfortune, but it is better to fear and tremble at it as appalling guilt. The more utterly wicked men become, the more
inevitable it is that they should sin; the vaster the mass of
a nation's sin becomes, as it rolls down through the centuries, the more inevitable is it that it will end in some
awful national crime. But, when the inevitable takes
place, it is an object not for pity only, but also for holy and
jealous wrath.

124. One thing about Jesus that from the first excited
their opposition to Him was the humbleness of His origin. Their eyes were dazzled with the ordinary prejudices
of the rich and the learned, and could not discern the
grandeur of the soul apart from the accidents of position
and culture. He was a son of the people; He had been a
carpenter; they believed He had been born in rude and

wicked Galilee; He had not passed through the schools of Jerusalem or drunk at the acknowledged wells of wisdom there. They thought that a prophet, and above all the Messiah, should have been born in Judaea, reared at Jerusalem in the center of culture and religion, and allied with all that was distinguished and influential in the nation.

125. For the same reason they were offended with the followers He chose and the company He kept. His chosen companions were not selected from among themselves, the wise and high-born, but were uneducated laymen, poor fishermen. No, one of them was a publican. Nothing that Jesus did, perhaps, gave greater offense than the choice of Matthew, the tax-collector, to be an apostle. The tax-collectors, as servants of the alien power, were hated by all who were patriotic and respectable, at once for their trade, their extortions, and their character. How could Jesus hope that respectable and learned men should enter a circle such as that which He had formed about Himself? Besides, He mingled freely with the lowest class of the population—with publicans, harlots, and sinners. In Christian times we have learned to love Him for this more than anything else. We easily see that, if He really was the Savior from sin, He could not have been found in more suitable company than among those who needed salvation most. We know now how He could believe that many of the lost were more the victims of circumstances than sinners by choice, and that, if He drew the magnet across the top of the rubbish, it would attract to itself many pieces of precious metal. The purest-minded and highest-born have since learned to follow His footsteps down into the depths of squalor and vice to seek and save the lost. But no such sentiment had up until His time been born into the world. The mass of sinners outside the pale of respectability were despised and hated as the enemies of society, and no efforts were made to save them. On the

contrary, all who aimed at religious distinction avoided their very touch as a defilement. Simon the Pharisee, when he was entertaining Jesus, never doubted that, if He had been a prophet and had known who the woman was who was touching Him, He would have driven her off. Such was the sentiment of the time. Yet, when Jesus brought into the world the new sentiment, and showed the divine face of mercy, the people ought to have recognized it. If their hearts had not been utterly hard and cruel, they would have leaped up to welcome this revelation of a diviner humanity. The sight of sinners forsaking their evil ways, of wicked women sobbing for their lost lives, and extortioners like Zaccheus becoming earnest and generous, ought to have delighted them. But it did not, and they only hated Jesus for His compassion, calling Him a friend of publicans and sinners.

126. A third and very serious ground of their opposition was that He did not Himself practice, nor encourage His disciples to practice, many ritual observances, such as fasts, punctilious washing of the hands before meals, and so forth, which were then considered the marks of a saintly man. It has been already explained how these practices arose. They had been invented in an earnest but mechanical age in order to emphasize the peculiarities of Jewish character and to keep up the separation of the Jews from other nations. The original intention was good, but the result was deplorable. It was soon forgotten that they were merely human inventions; they were supposed to be binding by divine sanction; and they were multiplied, until they regulated every hour of the day and every action of life. They were made the substitutes for real piety and morality by the majority; and to tender consciences they were an intolerable burden, for it was scarcely possible to move a step or lift a finger without the danger of sinning against one or the other of them. But no one doubted their authority, and the careful observance of them was reputed the badge of a godly life. Jesus regarded them as the great evil of the time. He therefore neglected them and encouraged others to do so; not, however, without at the same time leading them back to the great principles of judgment, mercy, and faith, and making them feel the majesty of the conscience and the depth and spirituality of the law. But the result was that He was looked upon as both an ungodly man Himself and a deceiver of the people.

127. It was especially in regard to the Sabbath that this difference between Him and the religious teachers was seen. In this area their inventions of restrictions and arbitrary rules had run into the most portentous extravagance, until they had changed the day of rest, joy, and blessing into an intolerable burden. He was in the habit of performing His cures on the Sabbath. They thought such work a breach of the command. He exposed the error of their objections again and again, by explaining the nature of the institution itself as "made for man," by reference to the practice of ancient saints, and even by the analogy of some of their own practices on the holy day. But they were not convinced; and, as He continued His practice in spite of their objections, this remained a standing and bitter ground of their hatred.

128. It will be easily understood that, having arrived at these conclusions on such low grounds, they were utterly disinclined to listen to Him when He put forward His higher claims—when He announced Himself as the Messiah, professed to forgive sins, and threw out intimations of His high relation to God. Having concluded that He was an impostor and deceiver, they regarded such assertions as hideous blasphemies, and could not help wishing to stop the mouth that uttered them.

129. It is surprising that they were not convinced by His miracles. If He really performed the numerous and stupendous miracles that are recorded of Him, how could they resist such evidence of His divine mission? The debate held with the authorities by the man whom Jesus cured of blindness, and whose case is recorded in the ninth chapter of John, shows how sorely they may sometimes have been pressed with such reasoning. But they had satisfied themselves with an audacious reply to it. It is to be remembered that among the Jews miracles had never been looked upon as conclusive proofs of a divine mission. They might be done by false as well as true prophets. They might be traceable to diabolical instead of divine agency. Whether they were so or not, was to be determined on other grounds. On these other grounds they had come to the conclusion that He had not been sent from God; and so they attributed His miracles to an alliance with the powers of darkness. Jesus met this blasphemous construction with the utmost force of holy indignation and conclusive argument; but it is easy to see that it was a position in which minds like those of His opponents might entrench themselves with the sense of much security.

130. They had early formed their adverse judgment of Him, and they never changed it. Even during His first year in Judaea they had pretty well decided against Him. When the news of His success in Galilee spread, it filled them with consternation, and they sent deputations from Jerusalem to act in concert with their local adherents in opposing Him. Even during His year of joy He clashed with them again and again. At first He treated them with consideration and appealed to their reason and heart. But He soon saw that this was hopeless and accepted their opposition as inevitable. He exposed the hollowness of their pretensions to His audiences and warned His disciples against them. Meanwhile they did everything to poison the public mind against Him; and they succeeded only too well. When, at the year's end, the tide of His popularity began to recede, they pressed their advantage, assailing Him more and more boldly.

131. They even succeeded early in arousing the cold minds of the Sadducees and Herodians against Him, no doubt by persuading them that He was fomenting a popular revolt that would endanger the throne of their master Herod, who reigned over Galilee. That mean and characterless prince himself also became His persecutor. He had other reasons to dread Him besides those suggested by his courtiers. About this time he had murdered John the Baptist. It was one of the meanest and foulest crimes recorded in history, a tragic instance of the way in which sin leads to sin, and of the malicious perseverance with which a wicked woman will compass her revenge. Soon after it was committed, his courtiers came to tell him of the supposed political designs of Jesus. But when he heard of the new prophet, an awful thought flashed through his guilty conscience. "It is John the Baptist," he cried, "whom I beheaded; he is risen from the dead." Yet he desired to see Jesus, his curiosity getting the better of his terror. It was the desire of the lion to see the lamb. Jesus never responded to his invitation. But just on that account Herod may have been more willing to listen to the suggestions of his courtiers, that he should arrest Him as a dangerous person. It was not long before he was seeking to kill Him. Jesus had to keep out of his way, and no doubt this helped, along with more important things, to change the character of His life in Galilee during the last six months of His stay there.

132. It had seemed for a time as if His hold on the mind and the heart of the common people might become so strong as to carry irresistibly a national recognition. Many movements, frowned on at first by authorities and dignitaries, has, by committing itself to the lower classes and securing their enthusiastic acknowledgment, risen to take possession of the upper classes and carry the centers of influence. There is a certain point of national consent at which any movement that reaches it becomes like a flood, which no amount of prejudice or official dislike can successfully oppose. Jesus gave Himself to the common people in Galilee, and they gave Him in return their love and admiration. Instead of hating Him like the Pharisees and scribes, and calling Him a glutton and a wine-bibber, they believed Him to be a prophet; they compared Him with the greatest figures of the past, and many, according as they were more struck with the sublime or with the melting side of His teaching, said He was Isaiah or Jeremiah risen from the dead. It was a common idea of the time that the coming of the Messiah was to be preceded by the rising again of some prophet. The one most commonly thought of was Elijah. Accordingly, some took Jesus for Elijah. But it was only a precursor of the Messiah they supposed Him to be, not the Messiah Himself. He was not at all like their conception of the coming Deliverer, which was of the most grossly material kind. Now and then, indeed, after He had performed some unusually striking miracle, there might be raised a single voice or a few voices, suggesting, Is this not He? But, wonderful as were His deeds and His words, yet the whole aspect of His life was so unlike their preconceptions, that the truth failed to suggest itself forcibly and universally to their minds.

133. At last, however, the decisive hour seemed to have arrived. It was just at that great turning point to which allusion has frequently been made—the end of the twelve months in Galilee. Jesus had heard of the Baptist's death, and immediately hurried away into a desert place with His disciples, to brood and talk over the tragic event. He sailed to the eastern side of the lake and, landing on the grassy plain of Bethsaida, went up a hill with the Twelve. But soon at its foot there gathered an immense multitude to hear and see Him. They had found out where He was, and gathered to Him from every quarter. Ever ready to sacrifice Himself for others, He came down to address and heal them. The evening came as His discourse continued, when, moved with a great compassion for the helpless multitude, He performed the stupendous miracle of feeding the five thousand. Its effect was overwhelming. The multitude became instantaneously convinced that this was none other than the Messiah, and, having only one conception of what this meant, they sought to take Him by force and make Him a king; that is, to force Him to become the leader of a messianic revolt, by which they might wrest the throne from Caesar and the princelings he had set up over the different provinces.

134. It seemed the crowning hour of success. But to Jesus Himself it was an hour of sad and bitter shame. This was all that His year's work had come to! This was the conception they yet had of Him! And they were to determine the course of His future action, instead of humbly asking what He would have them to do! He accepted it as the decisive indication of the effect of His work in Galilee. He saw how shallow were its results. Galilee had judged itself unworthy of being the center from which His kingdom might extend itself to the rest of the land. He fled from their carnal desires, and the very next day, meeting them again at Capernaum, He told them how much they had been mistaken in Him: they were looking for a bread king, who would give them idleness and plenty, mountains of loaves, rivers of milk, every comfort without labor. What He had to give was the bread of eternal life.

135. This discourse was like a stream of cold water directed upon the fiery enthusiasm of the crowd. From that hour His cause in Galilee was doomed; "many of his disciples went back and walked no more with him." It was what He intended. It was He who struck the fatal blow at His popularity. He resolved to devote Himself thereafter to the few who really understood Him and were capable of being the adherents of a spiritual enterprise.

THE CHANGED ASPECT OF HIS MINISTRY

136. Although the people of Galilee at large had shown themselves unworthy of Him, there was a considerable remnant that proved true. At the center of that group were the apostles; but there were also others, numbering probably several hundreds. These now became the objects of His special care. He had saved them as brands plucked from the burning, when Galilee as a whole deserted Him. For them it must have been a time of crucial trial. Their views were to a large extent those of the populace. They also expected a Messiah of worldly splendor. They had, indeed, learned to include deeper and more spiritual elements in their conception, but, along with these, they still held to traditional and material ideas. It must have been a painful mystery to them that Jesus should delay the assumption of the crown so long. So painful had this been to the Baptist in his lonely prison, that he began to doubt whether the vision he had seen on the bank of the Jordan and the great convictions of his life had not been delusions, and asked Jesus if He really was the Christ. The Baptist's death must have been an awful shock to them. If Jesus was the Mighty One they thought Him to be, how could He allow His friend to come to such an end? Still they held on to Him. They showed what it was that kept them by their answer to Him, when, after the dispersion that followed the discourse at Capernaum, He put to them the sad question, "Will ye also go away?" and they replied, "Lord, to whom shall we go? Thou hast the words of eternal life." Their opinions were not clear; they were in a mist of perplexities; but they knew that from Him they were getting eternal life. This held them close to Him, and made them willing to wait until He should make things clear.

137. During the last six months he spent in Galilee, He abandoned to a large extent His old work of preaching and miracle-working and devoted Himself to the instruction of these adherents. He made long trips with them to the most distant parts of the province, avoiding publicity as much as possible. Thus we find Him at Tyre and Sidon, far to the northwest; at Caesarea Philippi, on the far northeast; and in Decapolis, to the south and east of the lake. These journeys, or rather flights, were due partly to the bitter opposition of the Pharisees, partly of fear of Herod, but chiefly of the desire to be alone with His disciples. The precious result of them was seen in an incident that happened at Caesarea Philippi. Jesus began to ask His disciples what the popular views about Himself were, and they told Him the various conjectures that were flying about—that He was a prophet, that He was Elias, that He was John the Baptist, and so on. "But whom say ye that I am?" He asked; and Peter answered for them all, "Thou art the Christ, the Son of the living God." This was the deliberate and decisive conviction by which they were determined to stay with Him, whatever might come. Jesus received the confession with great joy, and at once recognized in those who had made it the nucleus of the future church, which was to be built on the truth to which they had given expression.

138. But this attainment only prepared them for a new trial of faith. From that time, we are told, He began to inform them of His approaching sufferings and death.

These now stood out clearly before His own mind as the
only issue of His career to be looked for. He had hinted as
much to them before, but, with that delicate and loving
consideration that always raised His teaching to their ca-
pacity, He did not refer to it often. But now they were in
some degree able to bear it; and, as it was inevitable and
near at hand, He kept insisting on it continually. But they
themselves tell us they did not in the least understand
Him. In common with all their countrymen, they expected
a Messiah who would sit on the throne of David, and of
whose reign there would be no end. They believed Jesus
was this Messiah; and it was to them utterly incom-
prehensible that, instead of reigning, He would be killed
on His arrival in Jerusalem. They listened to Him, they
discussed His words among themselves, but they regarded their apparent meaning as a wild impossibility.
They thought He was only using one of the parabolic
sayings of which He was so fond, His real meaning being
that the present lowly form of His work was to die and
disappear, and His cause rise, as it were, out of the grave
in a glorious and triumphant shape. He endeavored to
undeceive them, going more and more minutely into the
details of His approaching sufferings; but their minds
could not take the truth in. How completely even the best
of them failed to do so is shown by the frequent argu-
ments among them at this period as to who should in the
approaching kingdom be the greatest, and by the request
of Salome for her sons, that they should sit the one on the
right and the other on the left hand in His kingdom.
When they left Galilee and went up toward Jerusalem, it
was with the conviction that "the kingdom of God should
immediately appear"—that is, that Jesus, on arriving in
the capital, would throw off the guise of humiliation He
had up to this time worn, and, overcoming all opposition
by some show of His concealed glory, take His place on
the throne of His fathers.

139. What were the thoughts and feelings of Jesus Himself during this year? To Him also it was a year of sore trial. Now for the first time the deep lines of care and pain were traced on His face. During the year of successful work in Galilee, He was borne up with the joy of sustained achievement. But now He became, in the truest sense, the Man of Sorrows. Behind Him was His rejection by Galilee. The sorrow that He felt at seeing the ground on which He had bestowed so much labor turning out barren, is to be measured only by the greatness of His love to the souls He sought to save and the depth of His devotion to His work. In front of Him was His rejection at Jerusalem. That was now certain; it rose up and stood out constantly and unmistakably, meeting His eyes as often as He turned them to the future. It absorbed His thoughts. It was a terrible prospect; and, now that it drew near, it sometimes shook His soul with a conflict of feelings that we scarcely dare to picture.

140. He was very much in prayer. This had all along been His delight and encouragement. In His busiest period, when He was often so tired with the labors of the day that at the approach of evening He was ready to fling Himself down in utter fatigue, He would nevertheless escape away from the crowds and His disciples to the mountaintop and spend the whole night in lonely communion with His Father. He never took any important step without such a night. But now He was far oftener alone than ever before, presenting His case to His God with strong crying and tears.

141. His prayers received a beautiful answer in the Transfiguration. That glorious scene took place in the middle of the year of opposition, just before He left Galilee and set forth on the journey of doom. It was intended partly for the sake of the three disciples who accompanied Him to the mountaintop, to strengthen their faith and make them fit to strengthen their brethren. But it was chiefly intended for Jesus Himself. It was a great gift of His Father, an acknowledgment of His faithfulness up to this point, and a preparation for what lay before Him. It was about the death that was to take place at Jerusalem that He discussed with His great predecessors. Moses and Elias, who could thoroughly sympathize with Him, and whose work His death was to fulfill.

142. Immediately after this event He left Galilee and went south. He spent six months on His way to Jerusalem. It was part of His mission to preach the kingdom over the whole land, and He did so. He sent seventy of His disciples on before Him to prepare the villages and towns to receive Him. Again in this new field the same manifestations that Galilee had witnessed during the first months of His labors there showed themselves—the multitudes following Him, the wonderful cures, and so forth. We do not have records of this period sufficient to enable us to follow Him step by step. We find Him on the borders of Samaria, in Peraea, on the banks of the Jordan, in Bethany, in the village of Ephraim. But Jerusalem was His goal. His face was set like a flint for it. Sometimes He was so absorbed in the anticipation of what was to befall Him there, that His disciples, following His swift, mute figure along the highway, were amazed and afraid. Now and then, indeed, He would relax for a little, as when He was blessing the little children or visiting the home of His friends at Bethany. But His mood at this period was more stern, absorbed, and highly strung than ever before. His contests with His enemies were sharper, the conditions that He imposed on those who offered to be His disciples more stringent. Everything denoted that the end was drawing near. He was in the grip of His grand purpose of atoning for the sins of the world, and His soul was confined until it was accomplished.

143. The catastrophe drew near. He paid two brief visits to Jerusalem, before the final one, during His last six months. On both occasions the opposition of the authorities assumed the most menacing form. They sought to arrest Him on the first occasion, and they took up stones to stone Him on the second. They had already issued a decree that anyone acknowledging Him to be the Messiah should be excommunicated. But it was the excitement produced in the popular mind by the raising of Lazarus at the very gates of the ecclesiastical citadel that finally convinced the authorities that they could not satisfy themselves with anything short of His death. So they resolved in council. This took place only a month or two before the end came, and it drove Him for the time from the neighborhood of Jerusalem. But He retired only until the hour that His Father had appointed Him should strike.

7

THE END

144. At length the third year of His ministry verged toward its close, and the revolving seasons brought the great annual feast of the Passover. It is said that as many as two or three million strangers were gathered in Jerusalem on such an occasion. They not only flocked from every part of Palestine, but came over sea and land from all the countries in which the seed of Abraham was dispersed, in order to celebrate the event in which their national history began. They were brought together by various motives. Some came with the solemn thoughts and deep religious joy of minds responsive to the memories of the venerable occasion. Some looked forward chiefly to reunion with relatives and friends who had long been parted from them by residence in distant places. Not a few of the baser sort brought with them the cherished passions of their race, and were chiefly intent on achieving in so great a gathering some important business transaction. But this year the minds of tens of thousands were full of an unusual excitement, and they came up to the capital expecting to see something more remarkable than they had ever witnessed there before. They hoped to see Jesus at the feast, and entertained many vague forebodings as to what might happen with Him involved. His name was the word most often passing from mouth to mouth among the pilgrim bands that crowded the highways, and among the Jewish groups that talked together on the decks of the ships coming from Asia Minor and Egypt. Nearly all His own disciples no doubt were there, and were ardently cherishing the hope that at last in this gathering of the nation He would throw off the guise of humility that concealed His glory, and in some irresistible way demonstrate His messiahship. There must have been thousands from the southern portions of the country, in which He had recently been spending His time, who came there full of the same enthusiastic views about Him as were entertained in Galilee at the close of His first year there; and no doubt there were multitudes of the Galileans themselves who were favorably disposed toward Him and ready to take the deepest interest in any new development of His affairs. Tens of thousands from more distant parts, who had heard of Him but had never seen Him, arrived in the capital in the hope that He might be there, and that they might enjoy the opportunity of seeing a miracle or listening to the words of the new prophet. The authorities in Jerusalem, too, awaited His coming with mingled feelings. They hoped that some turn of events might give them the chance of at least suppressing Him; but they could not help fearing that He might appear at the head of a provincial following that would place them at His mercy.

THE FINAL BREACH WITH THE NATION

145. Six days before the Passover began, He arrived in Bethany, the village of His friends Martha, Mary and Lazarus, which lay half-an-hour from the city on the other side of the summit of the Mount of Olives. It was a convenient place to stay during the feast, and He took up His quarters with His friends. The solemnities were to begin on a Thursday, so on the previous Friday He arrived there. He had been accompanied the last twenty miles of His journey by a large multitude of pilgrims, to whom He was the center of interest. They had seen Him healing blind Bartimaeus at Jericho, and the miracle had produced among them extraordinary excitement. When they reached Bethany the village was ringing with the recent resurrection of Lazarus, and they carried the news to the crowds who had already arrived from all quarters in Jerusalem, that Jesus had come.

146. When, after resting over the Sabbath in Bethany, He arrived on Sunday morning to proceed to the city, He found the streets of the village and the neighboring roads thronged with a vast crowd, consisting partly of those who had accompanied Him on the Friday, partly of other companies who had come up behind Him from Jericho and heard of the miracles as they came along, and partly of those who, having heard that He was at hand, had flocked out from Jerusalem to see Him. They welcomed Him with enthusiasm, and began to shout, "Hosanna to the Son of David! Blessed is he that cometh in the name of the Lord! Hosanna in the highest!" It was a messianic demonstration such as He had formerly avoided. But now He yielded to it. He was probably satisfied with the sincerity of the homage paid to Him; and the hour had come when no considerations could permit Him any longer to conceal from the nation the character in which He presented Himself and the claim He made on its faith. But, in yielding to the desires of the multitude that He should assume the style of a king, He made it unmistakable in what sense He accepted the honor. He sent for an ass colt and, His disciples having spread their garments on it, rode at the head of the crowd. Not armed to the teeth or bestriding a war-horse did He come, but as the King of simplicity and peace. The procession swept over the brow of Olivet and down the mountainside; it crossed the Kedron and, mounting the slope that led to the gate of the city, passed on through the streets to the temple. It swelled as it went, great numbers hurrying from every quarter to join it; the shouts rang louder and more loud; the processionists broke off twigs from the palms and olives as they passed, and waved them in triumph. The citizens of Jerusalem ran to their doors and bent over their balconies to look, and asked, "Who is this?" to which the processionists replied with provincial pride, "This is Jesus, the prophet of Nazareth." It was, in fact, an entirely provincial demonstration. The Jerusalemites took no part in it, but held coldly aloof. The authorities knew only too well what it meant, and observed it with rage and dread. They came to Jesus and ordered Him to command His followers to hold their peace, hinting no doubt that, if He did not do so, the Roman garrison, which was stationed in the immediate vicinity, would pounce on Him and them, and punish the city for an act of treason to Caesar.

147. There is no point in the life of Jesus at which we are more urged to ask, What would have happened if His claim had been conceded—if the citizens of Jerusalem had been carried away with the enthusiasm of the provincials, and the prejudices of priests and scribes had been borne down before the torrent of public approval? Would Jesus have put Himself at the head of the nation and inaugu-

rated an era of the world's history totally different from
that which followed? These questions soon carry us beyond our depth, yet no intelligent reader of the Gospels
can help asking them.

148. Jesus had formally made offer of Himself to the
capital and the authorities of the nation, but met with no
response. The provincial recognition of His claims was
insufficient to carry a national assent. He accepted the
decision as final. The multitude expected a signal from
Him, and in their excited mood would have obeyed it,
whatever it might have been. But He gave them none,
and, after looking about Him for a little in the temple, left
them and returned to Bethany.

149. Doubtless the disappointment of the multitude
was extreme, and an opportunity was offered to the authorities that they did not fail to make use of. The
Pharisees needed no stimulus; but even the Sadducees,
those cold and haughty friends of order, perceived danger
to the public peace in the state of the popular mind, and
leagued themselves with their bitter enemies in the resolution to suppress Him.

150. On Monday and Tuesday He appeared again in
the city and engaged in His old work of healing and
teaching. But on the second of these days the authorities
stepped in. Pharisees, Sadducees and Herodians, high
priests, priests and scribes were for once combined in a
common cause. They came to Him, as He taught in the
temple, and demanded by what authority He did such
things. In all the pomp of official costume, of social pride
and popular renown, they set themselves against the simple Galilean, while the multitudes looked on. They entered into a sharp and prolonged controversy with Him
on points selected beforehand, putting forward their
champions of debate to entangle Him in His talk, their

distinct object being either to discredit Him with the audience or to elicit something from His lips in the heat of
argument that might form a ground of accusation against
Him before the civil authority. Thus, for example, they
asked Him if it was lawful to give tribute to Caesar. If He
answered Yes, they knew that His popularity would
perish on the spot, for it would be a complete contradiction of the popular messianic ideas. If, on the contrary, He
answered No, they would accuse Him of treason before
the Roman governor. But Jesus was far more than a match
for them. Hour by hour He stedfastly met the attack. His
straightforwardness put their duplicity to shame, and His
skill in argument turned every spear they directed at Him
around to their own breasts. At last He carried the war
into their own territory, and convicted them of such igno-
rance or lack of candor as to completely put them to shame
before the onlookers. Then, when He had silenced them,
He let loose the storm of His indignation and delivered
against them the bitter denunciation that is recorded in
the twenty-third chapter of Matthew. Giving unrestrained expression to the pent-up criticism of a lifetime,
He exposed their hypocritical practices in sentences that
fell like strokes of lightning and made them a scorn and
laughing stock, not only to the hearers then, but to all the
world since.

151. It was the final breach between Him and them.
They had been utterly humiliated before the people, over
whom they were set in authority and honor. They felt it to
be intolerable, and resolved not to lose an hour in seeking
their revenge. That very evening the Sanhedrin met in
passionate mood to devise a plan for doing away with
Him. Nicodemus and Joseph of Arimathea may have
raised a solitary protest against their precipitate proceedings, but they indignantly silenced them, and were
unanimously of the opinion that He should immediately

be put to death. But circumstances checked their cruel haste. At least the forms of justice would have to be gone through; and besides, Jesus evidently enjoyed an immense popularity among the strangers who filled the city. What might not the idle crowd do if He were arrested before their eyes? It was necessary to wait until the mass of the pilgrims had left the city. They had just with great reluctance arrived at this conclusion, when they received a most unexpected and gratifying surprise. One of His own disciples appeared and offered to betray Him for a price.

152. Judas Iscariot is the byword of the human race. In his *Vision of Hell* Dante has placed him in the lowest of the circles of the damned, as the sole sharer with Satan himself of the severest punishment; and the poet's verdict is that of mankind. Yet he was not such a monster of iniquity as to be utterly beyond comprehension or even sympathy. The history of his base and appalling lapse is perfectly intelligible. He had joined the discipleship of Jesus, as the other apostles also did, in the hope of taking part in a political revolution and occupying a distinguished place in an earthly kingdom. It is inconceivable that Jesus would have made him an apostle if there had not at one time been in him some noble enthusiasm and some attachment to Himself. That he was a man of superior energy and administrative ability may be inferred from the fact that he was made the treasurer of the apostolic company. But there was a cancer at the root of his character, which gradually absorbed all that was good in him and it became a tyrannical passion. It was the love of money. He fed it by the petty thefts from the small sums that Jesus received from His friends for the necessities of His company and for distribution among the poor with whom He was daily mingling. He hoped to give it unrestrained gratification when he became chancellor of the treasury in the new kingdom. The views of the other apostles were perhaps as worldly to begin with as his. But the history of their intercourse with their Master was totally different. They became ever more spiritual, he ever more worldly. They never, indeed, as long as Jesus lived, rose to the idea of a spiritual kingdom apart from an earthly one; but the spiritual elements that their Master had taught them to add to their material conception grew more and more prominent, until the earthly heart was eaten out of it, and merely the empty shell was left, to be in due time crushed and blown away. But Judas' earthly views became more and more engrossing, and were more and more divested of every spiritual adjunct. He grew impatient for their realization. Preaching and healing seemed to him a waste of time; the purity and unworldliness of Jesus irritated him; why did He not bring on the kingdom at once, and then preach as much as He chose afterward! At last he began to suspect that there was to be no kingom such as he had hoped for at all. He felt that he had been deceived, and began not only to despise but even hate his Master. The failure of Jesus to take advantage of the disposition of the people on Palm Sunday finally convinced him that it was useless to hold on to the cause any longer. He saw that the ship was sinking and resolved to get out of it. He carried out his resolution in such a way as to both gratify his master passion and secure the favor of the authorities. His offer came to them at just the right moment. They closed with it greedily, and, having arranged the price with the miserable man, sent him away to find a convenient opportunity for the betrayal. He found it sooner than they expected—two nights after the dastardly bargain had been concluded.

JESUS IN THE PROSPECT OF DEATH

153. Christianity has no more precious possession than the memory of Jesus during the week when He stood face to face with death. Unspeakably great as He always was, it may be reverently said that He was never so great as during those days of direst calamity. All that was grandest and all that was most tender, the most human and the most divine aspects of His character, were brought out as they had never been before.

154. He came to Jerusalem well aware that He was about to die. For a whole year the fact had been staring Him constantly in the face, and the long-looked-for had come at last. He knew it was His Father's will and, when the hour arrived, He bent His steps with sublime fortitude to the fatal spot. It was not, however, without a terrible conflict of feelings; the ebb and flow of the most diverse emotions—anguish and ecstasy, the most prolonged and crushing depression, the most triumphant joy and the most majestic peace—swayed back and forth within Him like the moods of a vast ocean.

155. Some have hesitated to attribute to Him anything of that shrinking from death that is natural to man; but surely without good reason. It is an instinct perfectly innocent; and perhaps the very fact that His bodily organism was pure and perfect may have made it stronger in Him than it is in us. Remember how young He was— only 33; the currents of life were powerful in Him; He was full of the instincts of action. To have these strong currents rolled back and the light and warmth of life quenched in the cold waters of death must have been utterly repugnant to Him. An incident that happened on the Monday caused Him a great shock of this instinctive pain. Some Greeks who had come to the feast expressed through two of the apostles their desire for an interview with Him. There were many heathens in different parts of the Greek-speaking world who at this period had found refuge from the atheism and disgusting immorality of the

times in the religion of the Jews settled in their midst, and
had accordingly become proselytes of the worship of
Jehovah. To this class these inquirers belonged. But their
application shook Him with thoughts they little dreamed
of. Only two or three times in the course of His ministry
does He seem to have been brought into contact with
representatives of the world lying outside the limits of His
own people, His mission being exclusively to the lost
sheep of the house of Israel. But on every such occasion
He met with a faith, a courtesy and nobility, which He
Himself contrasted with the unbelief, rudeness, and pet-
tiness of the Jews. How could He help longing to pass
beyond the narrow bounds of Palestine and visit nations
of such simple and generous disposition? He must often
have seen visions of a career like that afterward achieved
by Paul, when he bore the glad tidings from land to land,
and evangelized Athens, Rome, and the other great centers of the West. What joy such a career would have
caused to Jesus, who felt within Himself the energy and
overflowing benevolence that it would exactly have
suited! But death was at hand to extinguish all. The visit
of the Greeks caused a great wave of such thoughts to
break over Him. Instead of responding to their request,
He became abstracted, His face darkened, and His frame
was shaken with the tremor of an inward conflict. But He
soon recovered Himself, and gave expression to the
thoughts on which in those days He was steadying up His
soul: "Except a corn of wheat fall into the ground and die,
it abideth alone; but if it die, it bringeth forth much
fruit"; "And I, if I be lifted up from the earth, will draw all
men unto me." He could see beyond death, terrible and
absorbing as the prospect of it was, and assure Himself
that the effect of His self-sacrifice would be infinitely
grander and more extensive than that of a personal mission to the heathen world could ever have been. Besides,
death was what His Father had appointed for Him. This

was the last and deepest consolation with which He soothed His humble and trustful soul on this as on every similar occasion: "Now is my soul troubled; and what shall I say? Father, save me from this hour: but for this cause came I unto this hour. Father, glorify thyself."

156. Death approached Him with every terrible accompaniment. He was to fall a victim to the treachery of a follower of His own, whom He had chosen and loved. His life was to be taken by the hands of His own nation, in the city of His heart. He had come to exalt His nation to heaven, and had loved her with a devotion nourished by the most intelligent and sympathetic acquaintance with her past history and with the great men who had loved her before Him, as well as by the sense of all that He Himself was able to do for her. But His death would bring down the blight of a thousand curses on Palestine and Jerusalem. How clearly He foresaw that what was coming was shown by the memorable prophetic discourse of the twenty-fourth chapter of Matthew, which He spoke on Tuesday afternoon to His disciples, sitting on the side of Mount Olivet, with the doomed city at His feet. How bitter was the anguish it caused Him was shown on the Sunday, when, even in His hour of triumph, as the joyful multitude bore Him down the mountain road, He stopped at the point where the city burst on the view, and with tears and lamentations predicted its fate. It ought to have been the fair city's bridal day, when she should have been married to the Son of God; but the pallor of death was on her face. He who would have taken her to His heart, as the hen gathers her chicks under her wings, saw the eagles already in the air, flying fast to tear her in pieces.

157. In the evenings of this week He went out to Bethany; but in all probability He spent most of the nights alone in the open air. He wandered about in the solitude of the hilltop and among the olive groves and gardens with which the sides of the mount were covered; perhaps many times going along the same road down which the procession had passed and, as He looked across the valley, from the point where He had stopped before, at the city sleeping in the moonlight, startling the night with cries more bitter than the lamentation that overawed the multitude. Many times He may have repeated to His lonely heart the great truths He had uttered in the presence of the Greeks.

158. He was terribly alone. The whole world was against Him—Jerusalem panting for His life with passionate hate, the tens of thousands from the provinces turning from Him in disappointment. Not even one of His apostles, not even John, was in the least aware of the real situation, or able to be the confidant of His thoughts. This was one of the bitterest drops in His cup. He felt as no other person has ever felt the necessity of living on in the world after death. The cause He had inaugurated must not die. It was for the whole world, and was to endure through all generations and visit every part of the globe. But after His departure it would be left in the hands of His apostles, who were now showing themselves so weak, unsympathetic, and ignorant. Were they fit for the task? Had not one of them turned out a traitor? Would not the cause, when He was gone—so perhaps the tempter whispered—be destroyed, and all His far-reaching plans for the regeneration of the world vanish like the baseless fabric of a vision?

159. Yet He was not alone. Among the deep shadows of the gardens and on the summits of Olivet, He sought the unfailing resource of other and less troubled days, and found it still in His dire need. His Father was with Him;

and, pouring out supplications with strong crying and tears, He was heard in that He feared. He hushed His spirit with the sense that His Father's perfect love and wisdom were appointing all that was happening to Him, and that He was glorifying His Father and fulfilling the work given Him to do. This could banish every fear and fill Him with a joy unspeakable and full of glory.

160. At last the end drew very near. The Thursday evening arrived, when in every house in Jerusalem the Passover was eaten. Jesus also with the Twelve sat down to eat it. He knew that it was His last night on earth, and that this was His farewell meeting with His own. Happily there has been preserved to us a full account of it,. with which every Christian is familiar. It was the greatest evening of His life. His soul overflowed in indescribable tenderness and grandeur. Some shadows, indeed, fell across His spirit in the earlier hours of the evening. But they soon passed; and throughout the scenes of the washing of the disciples' feet, the eating of the Passover, the institution of the Lord's Supper, the farewell address, and the great high-priestly prayer, the whole glory of His character shone. He completely resigned Himself to the genial impulses of friendship, His love to His own flowing forth without limit; and, as if He had forgotten all their imperfections, He rejoiced in the anticipation of their future successes and the triumph of His cause. Not a shadow intercepted His view of the face of His Father or dimmed the satisfaction with which He looked on His own work just about to be completed. It was as if the Passion were already past, and the glory of His Exaltation was already breaking around Him.

161. But the reaction came very soon. Rising from the table at midnight, He and His disciples passed through the streets and out of the town by the eastern gate of the city and, crossing the Kedron, reached a well-known haunt of His at the foot of Olivet, the garden of Gethsemane. Here ensued the awful and memorable agony. It was the final access of the mood of depression that had been struggling all week with the mood of joy and trust whose culmination had been reached at the supper table. It was the final onset of temptation, from which His life had never been free. But we fear to analyze the elements of the scene. We know that any conception of ours must be utterly unable to exhaust its meaning. How, above all, can we estimate in the faintest degree the chief element in it—the crushing, scorching pressure of the sin of the world, which He was then expiating?

162. But the struggle ended in a complete victory. While the poor disciples were sleeping away the hours of preparation for the crisis that was at hand, He had thoroughly equipped Himself for it; He had fought down the last remnants of temptation; the bitterness of death was past; and He was able to go through the scenes that followed with a calmness that nothing could ruffle and a majesty that converted His trial and crucifixion into the pride and glory of humanity.

THE TRIAL

163. Jesus had just overcome in this struggle when through the branches of the olives He saw, moving in the moonlight down the opposite slope, the mass of His enemies coming to arrest Him. The traitor was at their head. Judas was well acquainted with his Master's haunt and probably hoped to find Him there asleep. For this reason he had chosen the midnight hour for his dark deed. It suited his employers well too, for they were afraid to lay hands on Jesus in the daytime, dreading the temper of the Galilean strangers who filled the city. But they knew how it would overawe His friends if, getting His trial over during the night, they could show Him in the morning, when the populace awoke, already a condemned criminal in the hands of the executors of the law. They had brought lanterns and torches with them, thinking they might find their victim crouching in some cave, or that they might have to pursue Him through the wood. But He came forth to meet them at the entrance to the garden, and they trembled like cowards before His majestic looks and withering words. He freely surrendered Himself into their hands, and they led Him back to the city. It was probably about midnight; and the remaining hours of the night and the early hours of the morning were occupied with the legal proceedings that had to be gone through before they could gratify their thirst for His life.

164. There were two trials, an ecclesiastical one and a civil one, in each of which there were three stages. The former took place, first before Annas, then before Caiaphas and an informal committee of the Sanhedrin, and, lastly, before a regular meeting of this court; the latter took place, first before Pilate, then before Herod, and, lastly, before Pilate again.

165. The reason for this double legal process was the political situation of the country. Judaea, as has been already explained, was directly subject to the Roman empire, forming a part of the province of Syria, and being governed by a Roman officer, who resided at Caesarea. But it was not the practice of Rome to strip those countries that she had subdued of all the forms of native government. Though she ruled with an iron hand, collecting her taxes with severity, suppressing every sign of rebellion with promptness, and asserting her paramount authority on great occasions, yet she conceded to the conquered as many of the insignia as possible of their ancient power.

She was especially tolerant in matters of religion. Thus the Sanhedrin, the supreme ecclesiastical court of the Jews, was still permitted to try all religious causes. However, if the sentence passed was a capital one, its execution could not take place without the case being tried again before the governor. So, when a prisoner was convicted by the Jewish ecclesiastical tribunal of a capital crime, he had to be sent down to Caesarea and prosecuted before the civil court, unless the governor happened to be in Jerusalem at the time. The crime of which Jesus was accused was one that naturally came before the ecclesiastical court. This court passed on Him a death sentence. But it did not have the power to carry it out. It had to hand Him on to the tribunal of the governor, who happened at the time to be in the capital, which he generally visited at the Passover.

166. Jesus was conducted first to the palace of Annas. This was an old man of seventy, who had been high priest a score of years before, and still retained the title, as did also five of his sons who had succeeded him, though his son-in-law Caiaphas was the actual high priest. His age, ability, and family influence gave him immense social weight, and he was the virtual, though not formal, head of the Sanhedrin. He did not try Jesus, but merely wished to see Him and ask a few questions; so Jesus was soon led away from the palace of Annas to that of Caiaphas, which probably formed part of the same group of official buildings.

167. Caiaphas, as ruling high priest, was president of the Sanhedrin, before which Jesus was tried. A legal meeting of this court could not be held before sunrise, perhaps about 6:00. But many of its members were already on the spot, those who had been drawn together by their interest in the case. They were eager to get to work, both to gratify their own dislike of Him and to prevent the interference of the populace with their proceedings. Accordingly, they resolved to hold an informal meeting at once, at which the accusation, evidence, and so forth might be put into shape, so that, when the legal hour for opening their doors arrived, there might be nothing to do but to repeat the necessary formalities and carry Him off to the governor. This was done; and while Jerusalem slept, these eager judges hurried to carry out their dark plot.

168. They did not begin, as might have been expected, with a clear statement of the crime with which He was charged. Indeed, it would have been difficult for them to do so, for they were divided among themselves. Many things in His life that the Pharisees regarded as criminal were treated by the Sadducees with indifference; and other acts of His, like the cleansing of the temple, which had enraged the Sadducees, afforded gratification to the Pharisees.

169. The high priest began by questioning Him as to His disciples and doctrine, evidently with the view of discovering whether He had taught any revolutionary tenets that might form a ground of accusation before the governor. But Jesus repelled the insinuation, indignantly asserting that He had ever spoken openly before the world, and demanded a statement and proof of any evil He had done. This unusual reply induced one of the minions of the court to strike Him on the mouth with his fist—an act that the court apparently did not rebuke, and which showed what amount of justice He could expect at the hands of His judges. An attempt was then made to bring proof against Him, a number of witnesses repeating various statements they had heard Him make, out of which it was hoped an accusation might be constructed. But it turned out a total failure. The witnesses could not

agree among themselves; and, when at last two were
found to unite in a distorted report of a saying of His early
ministry, which appeared to have some color of criminal-
ity, it turned out to be a thing so paltry that it would have
been absurd to appear with it before the governor as the
ground of a serious charge.

170. They were resolved on His death, but the victim
seemed to be slipping out of their hands. Jesus looked on
in absolute silence, while the contradictory testimonies of
the witnesses demolished one another. He quietly took
His natural position far above His judges. They felt it; and
at last the president, in a moment of rage and irritation,
commanded Him to speak. Why was he so loud and
shrill? The humiliating spectacle going on in the witness
box and the silent dignity of Jesus were beginning to
trouble even these consciences, assembled in the dead of
night.

171. The case had completely broken down, when
Caiaphas rose from his seat and, with theatrical solemnity, asked the question: "I adjure thee by the living God,
that thou tell us whether thou be the Christ the Son of
God." It was a question asked merely to induce Jesus to
incriminate Himself. Yet He who had kept silence when
He might have spoken now spoke when He might have
been silent. With great solemnity He answered in the
affirmative, that He was the Messiah and the Son of God.
Nothing more was needed by His judges. They unanimously pronounced Him guilty of blasphemy and worthy
of death.

172. The whole trial had been conducted with pre-
cipitance and total disregard of the formalities proper to a
court of law. Everything was dictated by the desire to
arrive at guilt, not justice. The same persons were both

prosecutors and judges. No witnesses for the defense were thought of. Though the judges were doubtless perfectly conscientious in their sentence, it was the decision of minds much earlier shut against the truth and possessed with the most bitter and revengeful passions.

173. The trial was now looked upon as past, the legal proceedings after sunrise being a mere formality, which would be finished in a few minutes. Accordingly, Jesus was given up as a condemned man to the cruelty of the jailers and the mob. Then followed a scene over which one would gladly draw a veil. An Oriental brutality of abuse broke forth on Him that makes the blood run cold. Apparently the Sanhedrists themselves took part in it. This Man, who had baffled them, impaired their authority and exposed their hypocrisy, was very hateful to them. Sadducean coldness could boil up into heat enough when it was really roused. Pharisaic fanaticism was inventive in its cruelty. They smote Him with their fists, they spat on Him, they blindfolded Him, and, in derision of His prophetic claims, commanded Him to prophesy who struck Him, as they took their turn of smiting Him. But we will not dwell on a scene so disgraceful to human nature.

174. It was probably between 6:00 and 7:00 in the morning when they conducted Jesus, bound with chains, to the residence of the governor. What a spectacle that was! The priests, teachers, and judges of the Jewish nation leading their Messiah to ask the Gentile to put Him to death! It was the hour of the nation's suicide. This was all that had come of God's choosing them, bearing them on eagles' wings and carrying them all the days of the past, sending them His prophets and deliverers, redeeming them from Egypt and Babylon, and causing His glory for so many centuries to pass before their eyes! Surely it was the very mockery of Providence. Yet God was not mocked. His designs march through history with resist-less tread, not waiting on the will of man; and even this tragic hour, when the Jewish nation was turning His dealings into derision, was destined to demonstrate the depths of His wisdom and love.

175. The man before whose judgment seat Jesus was about to appear was Pontius Pilate, who had been gover-nor of Judaea for six years. He was a typical Roman, not of the antique, simple stamp, but of the imperial period; a man not without some remains of the ancient Roman jus-tice in his soul, yet pleasure-loving, imperious, and cor-rupt. He hated the Jews whom he ruled, and, in times of irritation, freely shed their blood. They returned his hatred with cordiality, and accused him of every crime—maladministration, cruelty, and robbery. He vis-ited Jerusalem as seldom as possible; for indeed, to one accustomed to the pleasures of Rome, with its theaters, baths, games, and licentious society, Jerusalem, with its religiousness and ever-smoldering revolt, was a dreary residence. When he did visit it, he stayed in the magnificient palace of Herod the Great; it being common for the officers sent by Rome into conquered countries to occupy the palaces of the displaced sovereigns.

176. Up the broad avenue, which led through a fine park, laid out with walks, ponds, and trees of various kinds, to the front of the building, the Sanhedrists and the crowd that had joined the procession, as it moved on through the streets, conducted Jesus. The court was held in the open air, on a mosaic pavement in front of that portion of the palace that united its two colossal wings.

177. The Jewish authorities had hoped that Pilate would accept their decision as his own and, without going into the merits of the case, pass the sentence they desired. This was frequently done by provincial governors, especially in matters of religion, which as foreigners they could not be expected to understand. Accordingly, when he asked what the crime of Jesus was, they replied, "If he were not a malefactor, we would not have delivered him up unto thee." But he was not in the mood for concession, and told them that, if he was not to try the culprit, they must be content with such punishment as the law permitted them to inflict. He seems to have known something of Jesus. "He knew that for envy they had delivered him." The triumphal procession of Sunday was sure to be reported to him; and the neglect of Jesus to make use of that demonstration for any political end may have convinced him that He was politically harmless. His wife's dream may imply that Jesus had been the subject of conversation in the palace; and perhaps the polite man of the world and his lady had felt the discontent of their visit to Jerusalem relieved by the story of the young peasant enthusiast who was hooking the fanatic priests.

178. Forced against their hopes to bring forward formal charges, the Jewish authorities poured out a volley of accusations, out of which these three clearly emerged —that He had perverted the nation, that He refused to pay the Roman tribute, and that He set Himself up as a king. In the Sanhedrin they had condemned Him for blasphemy; but such a charge would have been treated by Pilate, as they well knew, in the same way as it was later treated by the Roman governor Gallio, when preferred against Paul by the Jews of Corinth. They had therefore to invent new charges, which might represent Jesus as formidable to the government. It is humiliating to think that, in doing so, they resorted not only to gross hypocrisy, but even to deliberate falsehood; for how else can we characterize the second charge when we remember the answer

He gave to their question on the same subject on the previous Tuesday?

179. Pilate understood their pretended zeal for the Roman authority. He knew the value of this vehement anxiety that Rome's tribute should be paid. Rising from his seat to escape the fanatical cries of the mob, he took Jesus inside the palace to examine Him. It was a solemn moment for Pilate, although he did not know it. What a terrible fate it was that brought him to this spot at this time! There were hundreds of Roman officials scattered over the empire, conducting their lives on the same principles as his was guided by, so why did it fall to him to bring them to bear on this case? He had no idea of the issues he was deciding. The culprit may have seemed to him a little more interesting and perplexing than others, but He was only one of hundreds constantly passing through his hands. It could not occur to him that, though he appeared to be the judge, yet both he and the system he represented were on their trial before One whose perfection judged and exposed every man and every system that approached Him. He questioned Him regarding the accusations brought against Him, asking especially if He pretended to be a king. Jesus replied that He made no such claim in the political sense, but only in a spiritual sense, as King of the Truth. This reply would have arrested any of the nobler spirits of heathendom who spent their lives in the search for truth, and was perhaps framed in order to find out whether there was any response in Pilate's mind to such a suggestion. But he had no such cravings and dismissed it with a laugh. However, he was convinced that, as he had supposed, there lurked nothing of the demagogue or messianic revolutionist behind this pure, peaceful, and melancholy face; and, returning to the tribunal, he announced to His accusers that he had acquitted Him.

180. The announcement was received with shrieks of disappointed rage and the loud reiteration of the charges against Him. It was a thoroughly Jewish spectacle. Many a time had this fanatical mob overcome the wishes and decisions of their foreign masters by the sheer force of clamor and persistance. Pilate ought at once to have released and protected Him. But he was a true son of the system in which he had been brought up—the statecraft of compromise and maneuver. Amidst the cries with which they assailed his ears he was glad to hear one that offered him an excuse for getting rid of the whole business. They were shouting that Jesus had excited the populace "throughout all Jewry, beginning from Galilee unto this place." It occurred to him that Herod, the ruler of Galilee, was in town, and that he might get rid of the troublesome affair by handing it over to him; for it was a common procedure in Roman law to transfer a culprit from the tribunal of the territory in which he was arrested to that of the territory in which he was living. Accordingly, he sent Him away, in the hands of his bodyguard and accompanied by His indefatigable accusers, to the palace of Herod.

181. They found this princeling, who had come to Jerusalem to attend the feast, in the midst of his petty court of flatterers and jovial companions, and surrounded by the bodyguard he maintained in imitation of his foreign masters. He was delighted to see Jesus, whose fame had so long been ringing through the territory over which he ruled. He was a typical Oriental prince, who had only one thought in life—his own pleasure and amusement. He came up to the Passover merely for the sake of the excitement. The appearance of Jesus seemed to promise a new sensation, of which he and his court were often sorely in want; for he hoped to see Him work a miracle. He was a man utterly incapable of taking a seri-

ous view of anything, and even overlooked the business
about which the Jews were so eager, for he began to
pour out a flood of rambling questions and remarks,
without pausing for any reply. At last, however, he
exhausted himself, and waited for the response of Jesus.
But he waited in vain, for Jesus did not give him one
word of any kind. Herod had forgotten the murder of the
Baptist, every impression being written as if on water in
his characterless mind; but Jesus had not forgotten it. He
felt that Herod should have been ashamed to look the
Baptist's Friend in the face; He would not stoop even to
speak to a man who could treat Him as a mere wonder-
worker, who might purchase His judge's favor by exhibiting his skill. He looked with sad shame on one who
had abused himself until there was no conscience or
manliness left in him. But Herod was utterly incapable of
feeling the annihilating force of such silent disdain. He
and his men of war treated Jesus with disdain, and,
throwing over His shoulders a white robe, in imitation
of that worn at Rome by candidates who were canvass-
ing for office, to indicate that He was a candidate for the
Jewish throne, but one so ridiculous that it would be
useless to treat Him with anything but contempt, sent
Him back to Pilate. In this guise He retraced His weary
steps to the tribunal of the Roman.

182. Then followed a course of procedure on the part
of Pilate by which he made himself an image of the time-
server, to be exhibited to the centuries in the light falling
on him from Christ. It was evidently his duty, when Jesus
returned from Herod, to pronounce at once the sentence
of acquittal. But, instead of doing so, he resorted to expe-
diency, and, being hurried on from one false step to
another, was finally hurled down the slope of complete
treachery to principle. He proposed to the Jews that, as
both he and Herod had found Him innocent, he should

scourge and then release Him; the scourging being a piece
of bread to their rage and the release a tribute to justice.

183. The carrying out of this monstrous proposal
was, however, interrupted by an incident that seemed to
offer to Pilate once more a way of escape from his
difficulty. It was the custom of the Roman governor on
Passover morning to release to the people any single prisoner they might desire. It was a privilege highly prized by
the populace of Jerusalem, for there were always in jail
plenty of prisoners who, by rebellion against the detested
foreign yoke, had made themselves the heroes of the
multitude. At this stage of the trial of Jesus, the mob of the
city, pouring from street and alley in the excited Oriental
fashion, came streaming up the avenue to the front of the
palace, shouting for this annual gift. The cry was for once
welcome to Pilate, for he saw in it a loophole of escape
from his disagreeable position. It turned out, however, to
be a noose through which he was slipping his neck. He
offered the life of Jesus to the mob. For a moment they
hesitated. But they had a favorite of their own, a noted
leader of revolt against the Roman domination; and besides, voices instantly began to whisper busily in their
ears, putting every art of persuasion into exercise in order
to induce them not to accept Jesus. The Sanhedrists, in
spite of the zeal they had manifested the hour before for
law and order, did not have enough scruples to take the
side of the champion of sedition; and they succeeded only
too well in poisoning the minds of the populace, who
began to shout for their own hero, Barabbas. "What,
then, shall I do with Jesus?" asked Pilate, expecting them
to answer, "Give us Him too." But he was mistaken; the
authorities had done their work successfully; the cry came
from ten thousand throats, "Let him be crucified!" Like
priests, like people; it was the ratification by the nation of
the decision of its heads. Pilate, completely baffled, an-

grily asked, "Why, what evil hath he done?" But he had put the decision into their power; they were now thoroughly fanaticized, and yelled back, "Away with him; crucify him, crucify him!"

184. Pilate did not yet mean to sacrifice justice utterly. He still had a move in reserve; but in the meantime he sent Jesus to be scourged—the usual preliminary to crucifixion. The soldiers took Him to a room in their barracks and feasted their cruel instincts on His sufferings. We will not describe the shame and pain of this revolting punishment. What must it have been to Him, with His honor and love for human nature, to be handled by those coarse men, and to look so closely at human nature's uttermost brutality! The soldiers enjoyed their work and heaped insult upon cruelty. When the scourging was over, they set Him down on a seat, and, finding an old cast-off cloak, flung it, in derisive imitation of the royal purple, on His shoulders; they thrust a reed into His hands for a scepter; they stripped some thorn twigs from a neighboring bush and, twining them into the rough semblance of a crown, crushed down their rending spikes on His brow. Then, passing in front of Him, each of them in turn bent the knee, while, at the same time, he spat in His face and, plucking the reed from His hand, smote Him with it over the head and face.

185. At last, having glutted their cruelty, they led Him back to the tribunal, wearing the crown of thorns and the purple robe. The crowds raised shouts of mad laughter at the soldiers' joke; and, with a sneer on his face, Pilate thrust Him forward, so as to meet the gaze of all, and cried, "Behold the man!" He meant that surely there was no use of doing any more to Him; He was not worth their while; could one so broken and wretched do any harm? How little he understood his own words! That

"Ecce Homo" of his sounds over the world and draws the eyes of all generations to that marred visage. And lo, as we look, the shame is gone; it has lifted off Him and fallen on Pilate himself, on the soldiery, the priests, and the mob. His outflashing glory has scorched away every speck of disgrace and tipped the crown of thorns with a hundred points of flaming brightness. But just as little did Pilate understand the temper of the people he ruled, when he supposed that the sight of the misery and helplessness of Jesus would satisfy their thirst for vengeance. Their objection to Him all along had been that one so poor and unambitious should claim to be their Messiah; and the sight of Him now, scourged and scorned by the alien soldiery, yet still claiming to be their King, raised their hate to madness, so that they cried louder than ever, "Crucify him, crucify him!"

186. Now at last they gave vent to the real charge against Him, which had all along been burning at the bottom of their hearts, and which they could no longer suppress: "We have a law," they cried, "and by that law he ought to die, because he made himself the Son of God." But these words struck a chord in Pilate's mind that they had not thought of. In the ancient traditions of his native land there were many legends of sons of the gods, who in the days of old had walked the earth in humble guise, so that they were indistinguishable from common men. It was dangerous to meet them, for an injury done them might bring down on the offender the wrath of the gods, their sires. Faith in these antique myths had long died out, because no men were seen on earth so different from their neighbors as to require such an explanation. But in Jesus Pilate had discerned an inexplicable something that affected him with a vague terror. And now the words of the mob, "He made himself the Son of God," came like a flash of lightning. They brought back out of the recesses of his memory the old, forgotten stories of his childhood, and revived the heathen terror, which forms the theme of some of the greatest Greek dramas, of committing unawares a crime that might evoke the dire vengeance of heaven. Might not Jesus be the Son of the Hebrew Jehovah—so his heathen mind reasoned—as Castor and Pollux were the sons of Jupiter? He hastily took Him inside the palace again and, looking at Him with new awe and curiosity, asked, "Whence art thou?" But Jesus did not answer him a word. Pilate had not listened to Him when He wished to explain everything to him; he had outraged his own sense of justice by scourging Him; and, if a man turns his back on Christ when He speaks, the hour will come when he will ask and receive no answer. The proud governor was both surprised and irritated, and demanded, "Speakest thou not to me? Knowest thou not that I have power to crucify thee, and have power to release thee?" to which Jesus answered with the indescribable dignity of which the brutal shame of His torture had in no way robbed Him, "Thou couldest have no power at all against me, except it were given thee from above."

187. Pilate had boasted of his power to do what he chose with his prisoner; but he was in reality very weak. He came forth from his private interview determined at once to release Him. The Jews saw it in his face; and it made them bring out their last weapon, which they had all along been keeping in reserve: they threatened to complain against him to the emperor. This was the meaning of the cry with which they interrupted his first words, "If thou let this man go, thou art not Caesar's friend." This had been in both their minds and his all through the trial. It was this which made him so irresolute. There was nothing a Roman governor dreaded so much as a complaint against him sent by his subjects to

the emperor. At this time it was especially perilous, for the imperial throne was occupied by a morbid and suspicious tyrant, who delighted in disgracing his own servants, and would kindle in a moment at the whisper of any of his subordinates favoring a pretender to royal power. Pilate knew too well that his administration could not bear inspection, for it had been cruel and corrupt in the extreme. Nothing is able so decisively to forbid a man to do the good he would do as the evil of his past life. This was the blast of temptation that finally swept Pilate off his feet, just when he had made up his mind to obey his conscience. He was no hero, who would obey his convictions at any cost. He was a thorough man of the world, and saw at once that he must surrender Jesus to their will.

188. However, he was full not only of rage at being so completely foiled, but also of an overpowering religious dread. Calling for water, he washed his hands in the presence of the multitude and cried, "I am innocent of the blood of this just Person." He washed his hands when he should have exerted them. Blood is not so easily washed off. But the mob, now completely triumphant, derided his scruples, rending the air with the cry, "His blood be upon us and on our children!"

189. Pilate felt the insult keenly and, turning on them in his anger, determined that he too should have his triumph. Thrusting Jesus forward more prominently into view, he began to mock them by pretending to regard Him as really their king, and asking, "Shall I crucify your King?" It was now their turn to feel the sting of mockery; and they cried out, "We have no king but Caesar." What a confession from Jewish lips! It was the surrender of the freedom and the history of the nation. Pilate took them at their word, and handed Jesus over to be crucified.

THE CRUCIFIXION

190. They had succeeded in wresting their victim from Pilate's unwilling hands, "and they took Jesus and led him away." At length they were able to gratify their hatred to the uttermost, and they hurried Him off to the place of execution with every demonstration of inhuman triumph. The actual executioners were the soldiers of the governor's guard; but in moral significance the deed belonged entirely to the Jewish authorities. They could not leave it in charge of the minions of the law to whom it belonged, but with undignified eagerness headed the procession themselves, in order to feast their vindictiveness on the sight of His sufferings.

191. It must by this time have been about 10:00 in the morning. The crowd at the palace had been gradually swelling. As the fatal procession, headed by the Sanhedrists, passed through the streets, it attracted great multitudes. It happened to be a Passover holiday, so there were thousands of idlers, prepared for any excitement. All those especially who had been inoculated with the fanaticism of the authorities poured forth to witness the execution. It was therefore through the midst of myriads of cruel and unsympathizing onlookers that Jesus went to His death.

192. The spot where He suffered cannot now be identified. It was outside the gates of the city, and was doubtless the common place of execution. It is usually called Mount Calvary, but there is nothing in the Gospels to justify such a name, nor does there seem to be any hill in the neighborhood on which it could have taken place. The name Golgotha, "place of a skull," may signify a skull-like knoll, but more probably refers to the ghastly relics of the tragedies happening there that might be lying about. It was probably a wide, open space, in which a multitude of spectators might assemble; and it appears to have been on the side of a much-frequented thoroughfare, for, besides the stationary spectators, there were others passing to and fro who joined in mocking the Sufferer.

193. Crucifixion was an unspeakably horrible death. As Cicero, who was well acquainted with it, says, it was the most cruel and shameful of all punishments. "Let it never," he adds, "come near the body of a Roman citizen; nay, not even near his thoughts, or eyes, or ears." It was reserved for slaves and revolutionaries whose end was meant to be marked with special infamy. Nothing could be more unnatural and revolting than to suspend a living man in such a position. The idea of it seems to have been suggested by the practice of nailing up vermin in a kind of revengeful merriment on some exposed place. Had the end come with the first strokes in the wounds, it would still have been an awful death. But the victim usually lingered two or three days, with the burning pain of the nails in his hands and feet, the torture of overcharged veins, and, worst of all, his intolerable thirst, constantly increasing. It was impossible to help move the body so as to get relief from each new attack of pain; yet every movement brought new and excruciating agony.

194. But we gladly turn away from the awful sight, to think how by His strength of soul, His resignation and His love, Jesus triumphed over the shame, the cruelty, and horror of it; and how, as the sunset with its crimson glory makes even the putrid pool burn like a shield of gold and drenches with brilliance the vilest object held up against its beams, He converted the symbol of slavery and wickedness into a symbol for whatever is most pure and glorious in the world. The head hung free in crucifixion, so that He was able not only to see what was going on beneath Him, but also to speak. He uttered seven sentences at intervals, which have been preserved to us. They are seven windows by which we can still look into His mind and heart, and learn the impressions made on Him by what was happening. They show that He retained unimpaired the serenity and majesty that had characterized Him throughout His trial, and exhibited in their fullest exercise all the qualities that had already made His character illustrious. He triumphed over His sufferings not by the cold severity of a Stoic, but by self-forgetting love. When He was fainting beneath the burden of the cross in the Via Dolorosa, He forgot His fatigue in His anxiety for the daughters of Jerusalem and their children. When they were nailing Him to the tree, He was absorbed in a prayer for His murderers. He quenched the pain of the first hours of crucifixion by His interest in the penitent thief and His care to provide a new home for His mother. He never was more completely Himself—the absolutely unselfish worker for others.

195. It was, indeed, only through His love that He could be deeply wounded. His physical sufferings, though intense and prolonged, were not greater than have been borne by many other sufferers, unless the exquisiteness of His bodily organism may have heightened them to a degree which to other men is inconceivable. He did not linger more than five hours—a space of time so much briefer than usual, that the soldiers, who were about to break His legs, were surprised to find Him already dead. His worst sufferings were those of the mind. He whose very life was love, who thirsted for love as the heart pants for the waterbrooks, was encircled with a sea of hatred and of dark, bitter, hellish passion, that surged around Him and flung up its waves about His cross. His soul was spotlessly pure; holiness was its very life; but sin pressed itself against it, endeavoring to force on it its loathsome contact, from which it shrank through every fiber. The members of the Sanhedrin took the lead in venting on Him every possible expression of contempt and malicious hate, and the populace faithfully followed their example. These were the men whom He had loved and still loved with an unquenchable passion; and they insulted, crushed, and trampled on His love. Through their lips the Evil One reiterated again and again the temptation by which Jesus had been assaulted all His life, to save Himself and win the faith of the nation by some display of supernatural power made for His own advantage. That seething mass of human beings, whose faces, distorted with passion, glared on Him, was an epitome of the wickedness of the human race. His eyes had to look down on it, and its coarseness, its sadness, its dishonor of God, its exhibition of the shame of human nature were like a sheaf or spears gathered in His breast.

196. There was a still more mysterious woe. Not only did the world's sin thus press itself on His loving and holy soul in those near Him; it came from afar—from the past, the distant and the future—and met on Him. He was bearing the sin of the world; and the consuming fire of God's nature, which is the reverse side of the light of His holiness and love, flamed forth against Him, to scorch it away. So it pleased the Lord to put Him to grief, when He who knew no sin was made sin for us.

197. These were the sufferings that made the cross appalling. After some two hours, He withdrew Himself completely from the outer world and turned His face toward the eternal world. At the same time a strange darkness overspread the land, and Jerusalem trembled beneath a cloud whose murky shadows looked like a gathering doom. Golgotha was nearly deserted. He hung silent for a long time amidst the darkness without and the darkness within, until at length, out of the depths of an anguish that human thought will never fathom, there issued the cry, "My God, my God, why hast Thou forsaken Me?" It was the moment when the soul of the Sufferer touched the very bottom of His misery.

198. But the darkness passed from the landscape and the sun shone again. The spirit of Christ, too, emerged from its eclipse. With the strength of victory won in the final struggle, He cried, "It is finished!" and then, with perfect serenity, He breathed out His life on a verse of a favorite psalm: "Father, into thy hands I commend my spirit."

THE RESURRECTION AND ASCENSION

199. There never was an enterprise in the world that seemed more completely at an end than did that of Jesus on the last Old Testament Sabbath. Christianity died with Christ, and was laid with Him in the sepulcher. It is true that when, looking back at this distance, we see the stone rolled to the mouth of the tomb, we experience little emotion; for we are in the secret of Providence and know what is going to happen. But when He was buried, there was not a single human being that believed He would ever rise again before the day of the world's doom.

200. The Jewish authorities were thoroughly satisfied of this. Death ends all controversies, and it had settled the one between Him and them triumphantly in their favor. He had put Himself forward as their Messiah, but had scarcely any of the marks they looked for in one with such claims. He had never received any important national recognition. His followers were few and uninfluential. His career had been short. He was in the grave. Nothing more was to be thought of Him.

201. The breakdown of the disciples had been complete. When He was arrested, "they all forsook him and fled." Peter, indeed, followed Him to the high priest's palace, but only to fall more ignominiously than the rest. John followed even to Golgotha, and may have hoped against hope that, at the very last moment, He might descend from the cross to ascend the messianic throne. But even the last moment went by with nothing done. What remained for them but to return to their homes and their fishing as disappointed men, who would be mocked during the rest of their lives with the folly of following a pretender, and asked where the thrones were that He had promised to seat them on?

202. Jesus had, indeed, foretold His sufferings, death, and resurrection. But they never understood these sayings; they forgot them or gave them an allegorical turn; and, when He was actually dead, these yielded them no comfort whatever. The women came to the sepulcher on the first Christian Sabbath, not to see it empty, but to embalm His body for its long sleep. Mary ran to tell the disciples, not that He was risen, but that the body had been taken away and laid she knew not where. When the women told the other disciples how He had met them, "their words seemed to them as idle tales and they believed them not." Peter and John, as John himself informs us, "knew not the Scripture, that he should rise from the dead." Could anything be more pathetic than the words of the two travelers to Emmaus, "We trusted that it had been he which should have redeemed Israel?" When the disciples met together, "they mourned and wept." There never were men more utterly disappointed and dispirited.

203. But we can now be glad they were so sad. They doubted that we might believe. For how is it to be accounted for, that a few days later these very men were full of confidence and joy, their faith in Jesus had revived, and the enterprise of Christianity was again in motion with a far vaster vitality than it had ever before possessed? They say the reason of this was that Jesus had risen, and they had seen Him. They tell us about their visits to the empty tomb, and how He appeared to Mary Magdalene, to the other women, to Peter, to the two on the way to Emmaus, to ten of them at once, to eleven of them at once, to James, to the five hundred, and so forth. Are these stories credible? They might not be, if they stood alone. But the alleged resurrection of Christ was accomplished by the indisputable resurrection of Christianity. And how is the latter to be accounted for except by the former? It might, indeed, be said that Jesus had filled their minds with imperial dreams, which He failed to realize; and that, having once caught sight of so magnificent a career, they were unable to return to their fishing nets, and so invented this story, in order to carry on the scheme on their own account. Or it might be said that they only fancied they saw what they tell about the Risen One. But the remarkable thing is that, when they resumed their faith in Him, they were found to be no longer pursuing worldly ends, but intensely spiritual ones; they were no longer expecting thrones, but persecution and death; yet they addressed themselves to their new work with a breadth of intelligence, an ardor of devotion, and a faith in results that they had never shown before. As Christ rose from the dead in a transfigured body, so did Christianity. It had put off its carnality. What effected this change? They say it was the Resurrection and the sight of the risen Christ. But their testimony is not the proof that He rose. The incontestable proof is the change itself—the fact that suddenly they had become courageous, hopeful, believing, wise, possessed with noble and reasonable views of the world's future, and equipped with resources sufficient to found the church, convert the world, and establish Christianity

in its purity among men. Between the last Old Testament
Sabbath and the time, a few weeks later, when this
stupendous change had undeniably taken place, some
event must have intervened that can be regarded as a
sufficient cause for so great an effect. The Resurrection
alone answers the exigencies of the problem, and is
therefore proved by a demonstration far more cogent than
perhaps any testimony could be. It is a happy thing that
this event is capable of such a proof; for, if Christ is not
risen, our faith is vain; but, if He is risen, then the whole
of His miraculous life becomes credible, for this was the
greatest of all the miracles; His divine mission is demon-
strated, for it must have been God who raised Him up;
and the most assuring glance that history affords is given
into the realities of the eternal world.

204. The risen Christ lingered on earth long enough to
fully satisfy His adherents of the truth of His resurrection.
They were not easily convinced. The apostles treated the
reports of the holy women with scornful incredulity;
Thomas doubted the testimony of the other apostles; and
some of the five hundred to whom He appeared on a
Galilean mountain doubted their own eyesight, and only
believed when they heard His voice. The loving patience
with which He treated these doubters showed that, though
His bodily appearance was somewhat changed, He was
still the same in heart as ever. This was pathetically shown
too by the places He visited in His glorified form. They
were the old haunts where He had prayed and preached,
labored and suffered—the Galilean mountain, the well-
beloved lake, the Mount of Olives, the village of Bethany
and, above all, Jerusalem, the fatal city that had murdered
her own Son, but which He could not cease to love.

205. Yet there were obvious indications that He belonged no more to this lower world. There was a new

reserve about His risen humanity. He forbade Mary to touch Him, when she would have kissed His feet. He appeared in the midst of His own with mysterious suddenness, and just as suddenly vanished out of sight. He was only now and then in their company, no longer according them the constant and familiar fellowship of former days. At length, at the end of forty days, when the purpose for which He had lingered on earth was fully accomplished and the apostles were ready in the power of their new joy to bear to all nations the tidings of His life and work, His glorified humanity was received up into that world to which it rightfully belonged.

CONCLUSION

206. No life ends even for this world when the body by which it has for a little been made visible disappears from the face of the earth. It enters into the stream of the ever-swelling life of mankind, and continues to act there with its whole force for evermore. Indeed, the true magnitude of a human being can often only be measured by what this life later shows him to have been. So it was with Christ. The modest narrative of the Gospels scarcely prepares us for the outburst of creative force that issued from His life when it appeared to have ended. His influence on the modern world is the evidence of how great He was, for there must have been in the cause as much as there is in the effect. It has overspread the life of man and caused it to blossom with the vigor of a spiritual spring. It has absorbed into itself all other influences, as a mighty river, pouring along the center of a continent, receives tributaries from a hundred hills. And its quality has been even more exceptional than its quantity.

207. But the most important evidence of what He was, is to be found neither in the general history of modern civilization nor in the public history of the visible church, but in the experiences of the succession of genuine believers, who with linked hands stretch back to touch Him through the Christian generations. The experience of myriads of souls, redeemed by Him from themselves and from the world, proves that history was cut in two by the appearance of a Regenerator, who was not a

mere link in the chain of common men, but One whom
the race could not from its own resources have produced
—the perfect Type, the Man of men. The experience of
myriads of consciences, the most sensitive to both the
holiness of the divine Being and their own sinfulness that
the world has ever seen, yet able to rejoice in a peace with
God that has been found the most potent motive of a holy
life, proves that in the midst of the ages there was
wrought out an act of reconciliation by which sinful men
may be made one with a holy God. The experience of
myriads of minds, rendered blessed by the vision of a
God who to the eye purified by the Word of Christ is so
completely Light that in Him there is no darkness at all,
proves that the final revelation of the Eternal to the world
has been made by One who knew Him so well that He
could not Himself have been less than divine.

208. The life of Christ in history cannot cease. His
influence grows more and more; the dead nations are
waiting until it reaches them, and it is the hope of the
earnest spirits that are bringing in the new earth. All dis-
coveries of the modern world, every development of more
just ideas, of higher powers, of more exquisite feelings in
mankind, are only new helps to interpret Him; and the
lifting up of life to the level of His ideas and character is
the program of the human race.

HINTS FOR TEACHERS
AND QUESTIONS FOR PUPILS

It will be observed that what has been attempted in the foregoing pages has been to throw into prominence the great time periods of our Lord's life, and point out clearly its main events, curtailing as much as possible details. These details are more popularly known than any other part of human knowledge; what most readers of the Gospels need is a plan with few details, in whose divisions they will naturally arrange themselves, so that the life may present itself to the eye as a whole; and an endeavor has here been made to supply this. But in a Bible-class course extending beyond twelve or fifteen lessons, more of the details might be introduced with advantage. There is therefore appended the outline of a more extended course, along with a few questions on the text intended to stimulate pupils to further thought and inquiry.[1]

PRELIMINARY

1. Characteristics of the four Gospels. *Matthew:* He-

---

[1]As a teacher's help I would recommend: (1) Andrews' *Bible Student's Life of our Lord,* an unpretentious but excellent book, in which the apologetic difficulties in the details of the life are treated with much candor and success; (2) Neander's *Life of Christ* (Bohn series), the best life, in my opinion, yet published, though sadly marred by too great concessions to the spirit of denial, which had reached its climax in Germany at the time when it was written; and (3) Farrar's, Geikie's or Edersheim's *Life of Christ,* which will lend vividness to the teacher's remarks. These books, along with a good commentary on the Gospels, a harmony of the Gospels, and a handbook of Bible geography, can be of great help.

brew thought and diction; well acquainted with Old Testament in the original; frequent quotations, "That it might be fulfilled"; aim to prove that Jesus was the Messiah; "the kingdom" very prominent; methodical groupings and combinations; groups of parables, chapters 13, 24, 25; of miracles, chapters 8, 9. *Mark:* Graphic and epic; supposed to be pupil of Peter, whose fiery spirit pervades his book; poetic objectivity and minuteness; details as to the looks and gestures of Jesus, the amazement He created, etc.; aim to show how He proved Himself to be the messianic King by a succession of astonishing deeds; stormful haste, "forthwith," "immediately," and the like, very frequent. *Luke:* More of the trained historian than the other evangelists; Hellenic grace of style; series of cameos; gives reasons of events; philosophic; psychological comments; Pauline spirit and universality; Christ not only for the Jews but for mankind; genealogy of Jesus traced back beyond Abraham. *John:* Supplies what the other evangelists omitted; dwells especially on the work of Jesus in Judaea; His private interviews; His interior life; His most profound and mysterious sayings; lyric fervor, profundity, and sublimity of farewell discourses. (See Lange, *Life of Christ,* i. 243–285, and article by Professor Bruce in *Catholic Presbyterian* for July 1879.)

2. When were our Gospels written? See Tischendorf's little pamphlet of this name (translation published by London Tract Society); Lange, vol. i.; or Weiss; Westcott on *The Study of the Gospels;* Salmon's, Weiss' or Dods' *Introduction to the New Testament.* It would probably be out of place in a Bible-class course to go to any length into this vexed and vast question. The most important point is the date of John's Gospel; see Luthardt, *St. John the Author of the Fourth Gospel* (Clark), or Watkins' *Modern Criticism considered in relation to the Fourth Gospel.* "The man who hides from himself what Christianity and the Christian revelation are takes the parts of it to pieces, and persuades himself that without divine interposition he can account for all the pieces. Here is something from the Jews and something from the Greeks. Here are miracles that may be partly odd natural events, partly nervous impressions, and partly gradually growing legends. Here are books, of which we may say that this element was contributed by this party, and the other by that, and the general colouring by people who held partly of both. In such ways as these Christianity is taken down and spread over several centuries. But when your operation is done, and the living whole draws itself together again, looks you in the face, refuses to be conceived in that manner, reclaims its scattered members from the other centuries back to the first, and re-asserts itself to be a great burst of coherent life and light, centring in Christ. Just so you might take to pieces a living tissue, and say there is here only so much nitrogen, carbon, lime, and so forth; but the energetic peculiarities of life going on before your eyes would refute you by the palpable presence of a mystery unaccounted for." (Principal Rainy, New College Inaugural Address, 1874.)

3. Other sources of the life of Jesus. References in Josephus, Tacitus, etc., of little moment except to show how small insight these observers had into the most important event of their times. Jewish history and antiquities explain the period. Ancient history exhibits "the fulness of time." Geography of Palestine.

4. The Annunciation. Prophecy of Baptist's birth. Visit of Mary to Elizabeth. Events connected with John's birth.

> 1. For what reasons may the life of Christ be regarded as the most interesting subject of human thought?

2. Why are the first three evangelists called the synoptists?
3. What is the meaning of the saying that the scenery of Palestine is the fifth Gospel?

CHAPTER 1

Paragraph 1. On the exact date of the birth of Jesus—probably 4 B.C.—see the essays at the beginning of Andrews' *Life*. Luke's statement that the taxing took place "when Cyrenius was governor of Syria" used to be pointed out as a mistake, Cyrenius having been governor ten years later; but the discovery that Cyrenius was twice governor (see Andrews, 3–6, 70–73) is a remarkable instance of how alleged mistakes in the Gospels are often made to disappear by further inquiry.

2. On the genealogies in Matthew and Luke, see Andrews.

3. On Bethlehem, see Stanley, *Sinai and Palestine*.

4. It has often been attempted to throw discredit on the story of our Lord's supernatural origin by comparing it to the heathen stories of how sons of the gods were born of mortal mothers; but, first, such an idea was utterly repugnant to the Jewish conception of God, and could not spring up on Jewish soil; and, secondly, even these stories, poured forth from the heathen mind, were indications of a deep sense in humanity of the need of the Incarnation.

9. On the star, see Andrews and Pressensé.

10. The Herods of the New Testament. 1. Herod the Great, in whose reign Jesus was born, reigned over the whole of Palestine; died very soon after Jesus' birth; his kingdom was divided at his death among his sons. 2. Herod Antipas, son of the former, was at his father's death made tetrarch of Galilee and Peraea; the murderer of the Baptist; Jesus was sent to him by Pilate. 3. Herod Agrippa I, grandson of Herod the Great, had as great dominions as he; put to death James, and imprisoned Peter; died miserably, as is related in Acts 12. 4. Herod Agrippa II, son of Agrippa I; Paul appeared before him, Acts 25.

Archelaus was soon deposed from the throne of Judaea, which became a part of the Roman province of Syria.

11. Farrar's chapter on the youth of Jesus is particularly good, and Geikie and Edersheim have many interesting remarks.

12. See *Apocryphal Gospels* in *The Ante-Nicene Christian Library*.

16. There are three opinions as to the brothers and sisters of Jesus: first, that they were His full brothers and sisters; second, that they were the children of Joseph by a former marriage; third, that they were His cousins. The Greek word for "brethren" is used with such latitude as to cover all these meanings. See the note in Plumptre's Introduction to the *Epistle of James*.

18. In Turpie's *Old Testament in the New* will be found much interesting information on the modes in which Christ and the apostles quote the Old Testament Scriptures, showing where they adhere literally to the Hebrew text, where to the Septuagint, and where they deviate from both.

20. When it is said at any point in His subsequent life that He retired to "the mountain," it is generally needless to inquire which mountain. It was any mountain that was accessible; there were few places in whose vicinity there was not mountainous land.

    9. To what extent must this star have been supernatural?

  18. What portions of Scripture were most quoted by Jesus? What is the Septuagint? What indications are there that Jesus did not generally speak on the spur of the moment, but thought His discourses carefully out beforehand?

  22. What views has Milton expressed on this subject in *Paradise Regained,* and what is their value?

CHAPTER 2

On the subjects treated in the first half of this chapter, the first 100 pages of Reuss' *Christian Theology in the Apostolic Age* will be found full of light.

27. It would be useful here to give a sketch of the history of the interval between the Old and New Testament histories, of which so little is popularly known. See Ewald's *History of Israel,* vol. v., or Stanley's *Jewish Church,* vol. iii, or Skinner's *Historical Connexion Between the Old and New Testaments.* On the various modes in which Rome ruled subject territories, see Ramsay's *Roman Antiquities,* pp. 131ff.

28. Synagogue arrangements, Farrar, i. 221ff. The ritual of Presbyterian churches is a close imitation of that of the synagogue, whereas Catholic ritual imitates that of the temple. See Dods' *Presbyterianism Older Than Christianity.*

30, 31. On the Pharisees, see Mozley's remarkable discourse in his *University Sermons.* Farrar, i. chap. 31, will supply useful illustration of what is said in the text in regard to the Scribes. A fund of information on these paragraphs in Hausrath's or Schürer's *New Testament Times*.

35. A somewhat lengthened lesson might here be introduced on the Old Testament prophecies and types. See Fairbairn's *Prophecy* and *Typology*.

38. I have not thought it necessary to describe the state of the world beyond Palestine; for, although the gifts that Jesus brought were for all mankind, yet His own activity was confined almost entirely to the house of Israel within its original home. In a history of early Christianity, or even a life of the apostle Paul, it would be necessary to extend our view over the whole disc of civilization that surrounded the Mediterranean, and in which the world's center, which has since shifted to other latitudes, was then to be found; and to show how marvelously, by the dispersion of the Jews through all civilized countries, the elementary conception of Christianity had been diffused beforehand far and wide; how the conquests of Alexander had, by making the Greek language universally understood, prepared a vehicle by which the gospel might be carried to all nations; how a pathway for it had been provided by the Roman power, whose military system had made all lands accessible; and, above all, how the decay of the ancient religions and philosophies, the wearing out everywhere of the old ideals of life, and the prevalence of heart-sickening sin, had made the world ready for Him who was the Desire of all nations. See chapter 5 of the author's *Life of St. Paul*.

26. What are the Apocrypha?
31, 32. Give parallels from the history of Christianity.
33. Compare the aspects of society in our country at present with those of Palestine in the time of Christ.

36. Give the names of persons who are said to have been waiting for the Messiah, and compile from the Song of Mary and elsewhere an outline of what their expectations were.
38. Compile from scattered references in the Gospels an outline of the conception which the scribes and the populace entertained of the Messiah and His era.

CHAPTER 3

45. John the Baptist, excellent subject for class essay.

49. Owen has a remarkable chapter on this subject in his work on the Holy Spirit (Book II. chap. 4).

50. *Potuit non peccare,* or *Non potuit peccare?* Ullmann, *Sinlessness of Jesus,* and *Christian Instructor* for 1830, pp. 1–96, and 118–224.

51. The official significance of the Temptation is explained in the text; but it would be well to give also its personal significance for the character of Jesus and His relation to His Father. Temptation to unbelief, presumption, and pride. Trench, *Gospel Studies.*

53. On the plan of Jesus, see Neander.

41. Give instances of men who have achieved a great life work in a short time and died young.
42. It has been maintained that Jesus changed His plan, because He first addressed Himself to the Jewish nation as a whole, but afterward organized the Christian church from the nucleus of a few disciples. What would you say in answer to such a view?
45. What was the difference between John's baptism and Christian baptism?
46. Some think that Jesus and John had met before: is it likely? On what grounds may it be supposed

that the dove and the voice from heaven were
perceived only by Jesus and the Baptist?
49. Collect the texts that speak of the influence of the
Holy Spirit on the human nature of Jesus.
53. Narrate Milton's account of the Temptation in
Paradise Regained.

What Andrews says on this subject, p. 109, is very
good and clear, and so are his characterizations of the
different periods, pp. 120, 167–173, 259, 296–301.

54. Sketch of the Geography of Palestine. See Stanley, *Sinai and Palestine;* Thomson, *The Land and the Book;*
Henderson's *Palestine* in this series; brief sketch in Farrar,
p. 52ff.

CHAPTER 4

59. There were two cleansings of the temple, the one
at the beginning and the other at the close of the ministry.
Such double accounts of similar events in the Gospels
have been seized upon as examples of the tendency in
speech to multiply one event into two. But it is forgotten
that this is a tendency not only of speech but of action,
and that when a person has done anything once, there is a
likelihood that he will do it again.

The Great Feasts: 1. The Passover, held in April, just
before the harvest began. 2. Pentecost, held fifty days
after the Passover, at the conclusion of the corn harvest
and before the vintage. 3. The Feast of Tabernacles, held
in autumn after all the fruits had been gathered in. 4. The
Feast of Dedication, which Jesus once attended, took
place in December.

57. Collect the sayings of John about Jesus, and of
Jesus about John.

CHAPTER 5

On Galilee, see Farrar, i. chap. 12. Neander's account of the means of Jesus is very valuable. For the convenience of teachers who may wish to follow in detail the incidents of each period, the following list of the events of this year may be given (see Andrews, pp. 198ff. and 536):

Second call of Peter, Andrew, James, and John.

Busy Sabbath: preaches in synagogue of Capernaum and cures demoniac; heals Peter's mother-in-law, and cures many after sunset.

Next morning goes to mountain to pray, then sets out on preaching tour in the neighboring towns, in one of which He cures a leper.

Returns to Capernaum; heals man "borne of four," forgiving his sins; accused of blasphemy; walks by seaside and teaches; calls Matthew; accused as Sabbath-breaker for allowing His disciples to pluck ears of corn and for healing withered hand on Sabbath.

Retires to a mountain; calls the Twelve; delivers the Sermon on the Mount.

Again in Capernaum; heals centurion's servant.

Another preaching tour; raises widow's son at Nain; receives message from Baptist and delivers panegyric on him; dines with Simon the Pharisee, and is anointed by the woman who was a sinner; parable of Two Debtors.

In Capernaum again; casts out dumb devil; visited by His mother and brethren; teaches from ship.

Crossing the lake, He stills a tempest; cures demoniacs in country of Gadarenes.

Back in Capernaum; Matthew's feast; raises Jairus' daughter and cures woman with issue of blood.

On another tour of the Galilean towns He revisits Nazareth; sends forth the Twelve; hears of Baptist's murder.

76. Some of the many questions in reference to the possibility and the proof of miracles would naturally, in an extended course, be treated here; see Mozley on *Mira-*

cles. There cannot, I think, be reasonable doubt that our Lord gave His sanction to the view that the demoniacs were actually possessed by evil spirits.

79. The acknowledgment that the Baptist wrought no miracles is a strong point against the mythical theory. If it was natural for that age, as this theory asserts, to surround persons who had impressed its imagination with a halo of miracle, why were not miracles attributed to the Baptist? Very few are narrated even of Paul.

80. Connection of the work of Christ with the fate of nature.

83. Monographs on our Lord's miracles by Trench, Bruce, Laidlaw, Steinmeyer.

84. On the teaching of Jesus many good remarks will be found in Harris' *Great Teacher*. On its parabolic form, Trench's introductory chapters in his *Parables* are good. A much fuller account of what Jesus taught than is given in the text would be very desirable in an extended course, and might be gathered from the relative portions of any of the handbooks of New Testament Theology (Weiss, Reuss, van Oosterzee, Schmidt). Monographs on the subject are Meyer's *Le Christianisme du Christ*, Bruce's *Kingdom of God* and Wendt's *Der Inhalt der Lehre Jesu*. On the Parables of our Lord there is a rich literature, e.g., Lisco, Trench, Arnot, Bruce, Dods, Taylor, Goebel.

92, 94, 100, 109–113. It would be a useful exercise for the members of a class to illustrate these paragraphs by abundant quotations from the Gospels.

98. See Candlish's Cunningham Lectures on *The Kingdom of God*.

103. Christ's method of dealing with inquirers.

105. On the apostolate, see Bruce, *Training of the Twelve*.

107. Sketches of the leading apostles. The difficulty about the choice of Judas is only a fragment of the larger difficulty of reconciling the foreknowledge of God and man's free will.

109. For some of the remarks on the character of Jesus I am indebted to Keim, *Geschichte Jesu*.

114. Ullmann's *Sinlessness of Jesus*.

115. Here the two names by which Jesus called Himself—Son of man and Son of God—should be explained. See Beyschlag's *Christologie*, Stanton's *Jewish Messiah*, or Baldensperger's *Selbstbewusstsein Jesu;* and an excellent article on the last two books by Rev. A. Halliday Douglas in *The Theological Review*, February, 1889.

76. Mention as many great and good men as you can who have been called mad.
77. What reasons may be suggested why Jesus sometimes used means and sometimes dispensed with them?
79. What proof of the credibility of the gospel account of the miracles of Christ is afforded by the confession that John worked none?
80. Is it correct to speak of the miracles of Jesus as interruptions of the order of nature?
81. What form of missionary effort seeks to imitate both the preaching and healing activity of Christ?
82. Can the popular notions about the wicked life of Mary Magdalene be proved from the Gospels to be incorrect?

83. With what evidence would you support the statement that Jesus, though the Man of Sorrows, was yet the most joyful of men?
86. What portions of the Old Testament especially justify this description of the Oriental mind?
89. Enumerate the parables of Jesus, and make a list of His other most remarkable figures of speech.
96. How would you account for the great difference between the circle of Christ's ideas recorded by the synoptists, and the circle of His ideas which we find in John?
97. Which of the evangelists uses the phrase, "the kingdom of heaven," and what does it mean?
103. Enumerate the private interviews of Jesus.
108. What proof of their Master's supernatural greatness is afforded by the character and achievements of the Twelve?
114. What conclusions can you draw from the fact that Jesus was sinless?
115. Prove the divinity of Christ as fully as possible from the first three evangelists, and show that it is a complete mistake to allege that it is taught only by the fourth of the evangelists.

CHAPTER 6

The events of this year were the following:

Leaving Capernaum, He crosses the lake; feeds five thousand; walks on sea; rescues sinking Peter.

Again in Capernaum; discourse on bread of life; many disciples forsake Him; He says that Judas has a devil; discussion about eating bread with unwashed hands.

Long journey to Tyre and Sidon, where He cures Syro-Phoenician woman's daughter; then to Decapolis, where He heals a deaf man and feeds four thousand; returns to Capernaum.

Leaves it again; cures blind man at Bethsaida; visits Caesarea Philippi; the great confession; the Transfiguration; cures demoniac boy; announces His death.

Again in Capernaum; pays tribute.

Visit to Jerusalem at Feast of Tabernacles; teaches in temple; attempt to arrest Him; Nicodemus seeks justice for Him; adulteress brought to Him; heals blind man, who argues with rulers; parable of Good Shepherd.

Final departure from Galilee.

Journey toward Jerusalem; John and James wish to rain fire on a Samaritan village; the Seventy sent out; journey through Peraea; parable of the Good Samaritan; the Lord's Prayer; dumb demoniac healed; encounters with Pharisees; parable of Rich Fool; "signs of the times"; heals infirm woman; warned against Herod.

At Feast of Dedication in Jerusalem; visit to Bethany; nearly stoned in the city.

Retires to Bethabara; while at a feast in a Pharisee's house on the Sabbath, heals dropsical man, and speaks parable of Great Supper; several parables directed against Pharisees.

Raising of Lazarus.

Retires to Ephraim; heals ten lepers; more parables against the Pharisees; blesses children; the rich young man; Salome's request; Jericho—Bartimaeus, Zaccheus; thence to Bethany.

Luke gives by far the fullest account of the events of the period between the final departure from Galilee and the final arrival at Bethany, chapters 9–19.

124–128. It would be a good exercise for the pupils to collect texts from the Gospels illustrating these paragraphs.

126. See Mackintosh's *Christ and the Jewish Law*.

136. The effect of the Baptist's death on the adherents of Jesus is put in a very striking, perhaps exaggerated way in *Philo-christus*.

143. At Feast of Tabernacles and Feast of Dedication.

122. How far does conscientiousness justify conduct? Illustrate your answer by historical parallels to the conduct of the Pharisees.

129. Can you show from the Old Testament that miracles were not necessarily evidences of a divine mission?

CHAPTER 7

Details not referred to in the text:

Supper at Bethany and anointing of Jesus by Mary; barren fig tree cursed; second purging of temple; widow's mites; several parables; details of parting meeting with the apostles; the portents that accompanied His death; details of His burial; restoration of Peter.

145. The Passover took place this year on April 6.

146. The anachronism of using the days of the Christian week will be condoned for the sake of clearness.

152. I cannot adopt the theory of Judas' career expounded in De Quincey's well-known and brilliant essay—that he thought Jesus too unworldly and hesitating, and precipitated Him into a position in which He would be compelled to exhibit His divine glory, but with no thought that He would suffer Himself to be executed. Its strong point is the suicide of Judas, which is held to have shown a kind of nobility in his nature. But it is inconsistent, I think, with his peculation and his kiss, and especially with the tone in which Scripture speaks of him.

156. Here an account might be given of the destruction of Jerusalem, to be gotten from Josephus.

160. On the difficult question whether it was the Paschal supper that Jesus ate with the apostles, and whether John places the crucifixion on the same day as the other evangelists, see Andrews, 368ff., and Farrar, Excursus x.; also an article by Rev. G. Brown in the *British and Foreign Evangelical Review* for October 1879.

169. The silence of Jesus.

172. On the legal aspects of the trial, see articles by A. Taylor Innes, Advocate, in *Contemporary Review*, August and October 1877.

180. Herod was ultimately banished to Gaul.

189. Pilate was also ultimately deprived of his position, and is said by Eusebius to have at length killed himself, "wearied with misfortunes." His wife, under the name of Claudia Procula, is included among the Catholic saints.

193. The cross was probably of the form in which it is familiarly represented, though sometimes it was like the letter T or the letter X. It raised the victim only a foot or two above the ground. The soldier was able to reach the lips of Jesus with a hyssop stalk.

195. The circumstance that blood and water flowed from His pierced side has been held by eminent medical authorities to prove that Jesus died literally of a broken heart—broken with sorrow. See the opinions of Sir J. Y. Simpson and other in the Appendix to Hanna's *Last Day of our Lord's Passion*.

199. With the argument of this section compare Paley, *Evidences of Christianity*, Part i.

201. Details of Peter's fall. It was when passing from the committee room, where He had been informally tried, to a barrack room, where He was detained until the legal hour for opening the court arrived, that "Jesus turned and looked upon Peter."

203. In some ways the most important appearance of all may have been that to His own brother James. On its results and their apologetic value, see *Imago Christi*, p. 50.

144. Quote a passage from Acts to show from how many different countries the scattered Jews gathered to the annual feast.
147. The meaning of Hosanna and of Hallelujah?
155. Who were the persons not of Abraham's seed with whom Jesus came in contact in the course of His ministry?
163. Collect the texts in which the majesty of our Lord's appearance is mentioned.
181. In what points was the trial of Paul that resulted in his being sent to Rome similar to that of Jesus?
194. What were the seven last sentences of Jesus?
203. What is the meaning of the remark, that the Christian church is the best biography of Christ?